Contents

Acknowledgments vii

Priceless Pearls 1

Faith
    Bubbles of Truth 5
    Clean Hearts 7
    Endless Ripples 8
    Faith…in a Basement 10
    Hand in Hand 12
    My Hand in His 14
    Seeing Through the Fog 16
    Simply by Faith 18
    Through a Child's Eyes 20
    Trust Him 22

Grace
    Baskets and Washboards 27
    Come As You Are 29
    Faithful and Unchanging 31
    He Changes Not 33
    Indescribable Grace 35
    Marvelous Grace 37
    Now is the Time 39
    Standing Firm 41
    Throwing Rocks 43

Hope
- An Anchor of Hope 47
- But God 49
- Follow the "Sonlight" 51
- Hearts of Life 53
- Resisting the Attack 55
- The Pot and the Potter 57
- Water of Hope 59

Living a Christian Life
- Dare to be Red 63
- Feasting on Solid Food 65
- Look to the Light 67
- Sifted and Worthy 69

Love
- Are You a Scorekeeper? 73
- As God's Hands 75
- On Business for Our King 77
- Strand of Love 79
- The Cardinal's Reminder 80

Mercy
- A Confident Approach 85
- Clean and Unspotted 87
- Favor and Freon 89
- From Death to Life 91
- Grip Before You Slip 92
- Splinter of Sin 94
- The Dark Well 96

Peace
- Can You Hear? 101
- Do Not Fear 103
- In His Shadow 105
- The Gift of Life 107
- Who Am I? 109

Promises
- Balancing Priorities 113
- Deeply Rooted 115
- Deflecting Satan's Arrows 117
- God is Always God..119
- Guidance, Courtesy of God..121
- Over the Rainbow...123
- Protection in the Shade 125
- Taste and See..127
- Truly Committed 129

Salvation
- Enter the Narrow Gate...133
- Granddaddy's Jesus...135
- Heaven or Hell?..137
- Your Name, Not a Blank 139

Acknowledgments

There are many people that I need to thank for their help and support in making *Pearls of Great Price* possible.

My husband, Brooks, for supporting my desire and my calling to write and for being my guinea pig that read a draft of a devotion before anyone else. This sometimes even meant supper was late!

My children, Blair and Gregory, for their love and support and for allowing me to use their children, Amelia and Bryson, in most of my devotionals.

My sister in Christ and prayer partner, Kathy Crouch, for encouraging and uplifting me as she herself was writing her book and busy with her own publishing process. Kathy's poem "Precious Pearls" begins this work, just as her poem "The Pond" introduced my book of the same title back in 2016.

My friend and sister in Christ, Jan Allen, for creating the cover artwork that adorns the front cover of this book. She has used her gift to create covers for two other books that had been published through Christian Faith Publishing by the members of our church, Crestview Baptist.

My pastor, Robby Stewart, for advice and help in proofreading my rough draft. Robby has been an encourager and always ready to help. He is a wealth of wisdom and knowledge, and I am grateful to have him as my pastor.

Finally, my fellow church members at Crestview and those outside my church family, who read each devotion as it appeared on our church webpage and offered comments of encouragement.

LUCY ALLEN

It takes a village to produce a writer through support, encouragement, and, most of all, prayer. Thank you all for being my village, and thanks be to God for choosing me to write His words.

Priceless Pearls

Come walk with me
Beyond the pond
Through all of nature
In search for the kingdom
As a precious Jewel

The kingdom of heaven
Like unto a merchant
Seeking goodly pearls
Come walk with me
You'll see

Priceless
Precious
To the one who finds them

Pearls of…
Faith
Grace
Hope
Love and mercy

All pointing to the cross
The cross of Calvary
Security for the soul

LUCY ALLEN

Seeking Salvation——
More valuable than pearls

Come walk with me
Through all of nature
In search for the kingdom

Kathy M. Crouch

Faith

Bubbles of Truth

My grandson and I were blowing bubbles late one afternoon with the sun in just the right position to create iridescence within each bubble. This is caused by the light reflecting off the front and back of the bubble. As the bubbles floated on the wind, some going into the woods and others travelling out over the pond, they brought to mind the bubble in which Glinda, the good witch of the North, arrived in in Munchkinland. Good witches and fairy godmothers are portrayed in so many children's books, and I would guess that most of us, as children, wished we had a fairy godmother to grant all our wants and wishes! We however have something so much better! We have a heavenly Father that loves and wants a relationship with each and every one! Unlike the make-believe granters of wishes and fixers of problems, He is real! Psalm 90:2 says, "Before the mountains were born, before you birthed the earth and the inhabited world-from forever in the past to forever in the future, you are God." What a beautiful picture!

Let's start at the very beginning with Genesis 1:1: "In the beginning God" (KJV) tells us that God has always been present. There is also this verse from Romans 1:20 that explains there is no excuse for unbelief: "Ever since the creation of the world, God's invisible qualities—God's eternal power and divine nature—have been clearly seen, because they are understood through the things God has made. So humans are without excuse."

Our God is Creator, giver, and sustainer of life. We know that every good and perfect gift is provided from the Father (James 1:17). He is the lover of our souls, our protector, and so much more! So how do we know this God when we cannot see Him? We know Him through His Son, Jesus, as we read in John 1:18, "No one has ever seen God. God the only Son, who is at the Father's side, has made God known." Jesus personified God the Father while He was on earth, and He said, "If you have seen me, you have seen the Father" (John 14:9). And we find in John 10:30: "I and the Father are one."

> *Is God real and does He care—*
> *Or is trust in Him like bubbles on the air?*
> *So beautiful and magical when first they are blown—*
> *Is that how you feel, that God is just an unknown?*
> *Drop your bubble wand and take a stand—*
> *Reach out, take His hand…allow Him to show you the way,*
> *To trust and believe forever and a day.*

Today is the day to put your trust and hope in Jesus and realize how very real He is!

Clean Hearts

A dead pine tree stands at the edge of the pond in stark contrast to the surrounding trees. You see, this tree stands stripped of its bark and pine needles; the heart of the tree itself is white, as if it's been bleached by the sun.

While I sat outside, contemplating this naked tree, I was reminded of how God sees us. He sees us without the trappings of the world. He sees directly into our hearts. In fact, we read in Proverbs 21:2, "Every way of a man is right in his own eyes: but the Lord pondereth the hearts." So what exactly does it mean to ponder? *Webster's Dictionary* tells us that to ponder means (1) to weigh in the mind: appraise and (2) to think about: reflect on. That's a scary thought for me! Do I really want God to appraise or reflect on what's on my heart? As much as I desire a heart that God can look upon without grimacing, I will never have it apart from Him. Jeremiah 17:9 confirms it, *"The heart is deceitful above all things, and desperately wicked: who can know it?"*

"A broken and contrite heart, O God, thou wilt not despise"— David prayed this in Psalm 51:17. He begged God to accept his broken and shattered heart as his sacrifice. If we follow David's example and sincerely offer our broken, dirty, and deceitful heart to Jesus, He will be faithful to accept our sacrifice and wipe our hearts clean.

In closing, I invite you to pray the following with me today:

> Create in me a clean heart, O God; and
> renew a right spirit within me. (Psalm 51:10)

Endless Ripples

From the spot the pebble hit the water, the ripples expanded across the surface of the pond. Ever widening, the concentric circles were hypnotic and set my mind in motion. Our lives are like those ripples, reaching out from each of us and touching people we know and, sometimes, those we do not know. As Christians, our lives should show a life lived for Christ. In living in such a manner, we have an effect on anyone we come in contact with.

We do not always see that last ripple that forms from the thrown pebble. In the same way, we will not always know how people we have come in contact with have responded to the example we showed them. How others are touched by our actions or words, we may not know until we see those results in heaven.

What we do know is this: "We are God's accomplishment, created in Christ Jesus to do good things. God planned for these good things to be the way that we live our lives" (Ephesians 2:10). It is an enormous responsibility when I think I portray the gospel in what I say and do. Our job is to continually cast ourselves upon the water and put in motion those ripples that God can direct toward others, saved or unsaved.

In my thoughts of water and rock, I found myself considering the idea of Christ as a rock, as I mentioned in a separate devotion. Not only is He a rock, our rock; look at His arrival on earth and what a ripple His life produced and still produces! Christ is the ripple of all ripples; His life and ministry continues to reach people today!

The influence, that expanding ripple that God has begun in your life, can affect many: friends, family, coworkers, neighbors, and strangers.

What kind of ripples are you setting into motion by words and works for Christ? You may not see the shore on which each rippling wave lands, but the shore where you stand right now is where the ripple begins.

This thought shared with me by my pastor is a great reminder with which to close this devotion: "God very seldom blesses us for our own benefit. He blesses us for the benefit of others!"

Faith...in a Basement

The house my children grew up in had a full, finished basement, and that is where my husband's workshop was housed. Over the years, this became the place where anything that was in need of repair went...down to the basement. Whether it was a broken lamp, bookcase. or toy, my husband took it downstairs. When it came back upstairs, it was fixed! I must add here that my husband is an engineer and seems to be able to figure out how to repair most anything.

One day, having a conversation with my son, who was probably six or seven years old at the time, about the things Daddy took into the basement and came back to him fixed, he made the statement, "if I broke my arm, Daddy could take me to the basement and fix it." Oh, the innocence of children! They are so trusting, and what faith they have in us as parents.

This is the kind of faith we, as Christians, need: the faith of a child. In Luke 18, we read of Jesus blessing the children, and in verse 17, He tells us, "Verily I say unto you, Whosoever shall not receive the kingdom of God as little child shall in no wise enter therein." Just as my son trusted his earthly father, we must learn to trust our heavenly Father. It is by faith that we place our trust in Him.

The *Believer's Bible Commentary* puts it this way: Little children do not need to become adults in order to be saved, but adults do need the simple faith and humility of a little child in order to enter God's kingdom.

Father God,
Grow my faith daily into that of a child's
That I may enter Your kingdom.
Help me to run to you as a child runs
To his parents for assurance.
Remind me that Your arms are open wide enough to
Cover me under your wings and be my shield
And buckler.
Amen.

Hand in Hand

Let me set the scene for you…my front yard, between 9:30–10:00 a.m., most mornings, you will find me playing trucks, digging in the sand, or kicking ball with my grandson, Bryson. In addition to the playtime, I take advantage of the time to tell him Who created, well, everything. We look at bird feathers, acorns, pine cones, and any other things that pop up. An important detail of being outside is that he always reaches for my hand to lead and guide him. He does not hesitate to take my hand when I offer it. Today, God nudged my mind to realize how He also offers a hand. Sadly, too often, we do not grasp it in return.

The Father's desire is that we take His hand in faith and dependence, just as a toddler grabs ahold of his parent's hand. I wonder how many times He reached out to me that I didn't recognize or acknowledge it. The Bible tells us that we are to have faith as a child, and that involves His hand holding mine.

I have in my mind the image of Christ on the cross with hands outstretched, a pleading in His eyes for each and every one to take hold of that nail-scarred hand.

We find in Psalm 89:13–15 the following: "Thou hast a mighty arm: strong is thy hand, and high is thy right hand. Justice and judgment are the habitation of thy throne: mercy and truth go before thy face. Blessed is the people that know the joyful sound: they shall walk, O Lord, in the light of thy countenance." Oh, where else would you rather be than walking hand in hand with Jesus?

Raising our hand to take His is a simple response to a simple gesture that means more than life! It is life! Take the hand that

Jesus offers, and walk with Him day by day in the light of His countenance!

This quote by Minnie Louise Haskins from the poem "The Gate of the Year" is a good way to conclude today's devotion:

> Go out into the darkness and put your hand into the Hand of God. That shall be to you better than light and safer than a known way.

My Hand in His

On a recent afternoon, one warm enough to allow a little time outside, my grandson and I walked up to our mailbox. As we started out, I extended my hand to him, and without hesitation, he placed his little hand in mine. The sun was warm on our heads, so we took our time checking out all the sticks, pine cones, and rocks along the way. When we got near a tree, however, he pulled his hand away and went off on his own to investigate each tree. The important thing is, each time, he made his way back to me and continued holding my hand. As long as I had a hold of that little hand, I could guide him in the way I wanted to go with him. Is this picture bringing anything to your mind as it did for me?

Our excursion experience brought to mind the scripture from Matthew 7:13–14: "Go in through the narrow gate. The gate that leads to destruction is broad and the road wide, so many people enter through it. But the gate that leads to life is narrow and the road difficult, so few people find it." We must keep our hand in Jesus's hand to navigate the narrow and difficult road of life.

How Christ wants to be our hand-holder! So often we are gladly willing to place our hand into His nail-scarred one, only to pull away when something comes along and catches our attention. We do as my little grandson did, slipping his hand out of my grasp to go his own way, making his own path. If we will only make our way back, we will find His hand is always extended! It is up to us to maintain contact!

The chorus of the hymn "Put Your Hand in the Hand of Jesus" is a great little reminder of this truth.

PEARLS OF GREAT PRICE

Put your hand in the hand of Jesus. Hold it tight and don't let go. Put your hand in the hand of Jesus, Follow! Follow Him where're He goes. (David Holder)

Seeing Through the Fog

Upon waking this morning, I sat up to be able to see out through the bay window. Gray, just gray—that was my first thought. Gray it was, for there was a thick fog blanketing everything. I could not even see the pond, just a few feet away. As I lay there, trying unsuccessfully to see my outdoor surroundings, I realized that the window itself was wet with condensation, and the rivulets of water drizzling down the glass made me think of tears, tears streaking down. Oh, what a sad and gloomy day this had dawned to be! How easy it would be to drag myself out of bed and mope around all day in a mood as gray as the fog.

I think we have two ideas here. First let's think about seeing through the fog; or maybe I should say *not* seeing through the fog. This makes me consider how sometimes we don't see God or see how He may be working in a particular situation. Often we assume, if we can't see something, it doesn't exist. Just as I looked out the window this morning, even though I was not able to see the pond, I knew it was there. Through the fog of life, if we are trusting in God and believing His word, our faith will assure us that He is there...always. Jeremiah 23:23–24 tells us, "Am I a God at hand, declares the Lord, and not a God far away? Can a man hide himself in secret places so that I cannot see him? Declares the Lord. Do I not fill heaven and earth? Declares the Lord." This tells me that, in the midst of the thickest of fogs, God sees me even when my eyes can't see Him.

The second point I want to look at is the gloom that is painted in the description of the day. In the darkest of days, we, as members of God's family, can be joyful. It's important to remember that by knowing Christ, joy is available when happiness may not be. Being secure in our salvation creates joy in the heart! One example comes from 1 Peter 1:8: "Though you have not seen him, you love him. Though you do not now see him, you believe in him and rejoice with joy that is inexpressible and filled with glory." No matter the condition of the day, we are instructed in Psalm 118:24 that we are to rejoice and be glad in the day, for the Lord has made it.

Both thoughts can be tied together to teach us that no matter how thick the fog in which we may find ourselves or how gloomy the day, God is always there, and in Christ, we have our joy.

Corrie Ten Boom says it this way: "Faith is like radar that sees through the fog—the reality of things at a distance that the human eye cannot see."

Faith and joy, cause and effect—faith is the cause; joy is the result.

Simply by Faith

My husband and I decided to put the small pond boat on the water and meander around the pond while he fished off and on. It was a late summer afternoon on the pond. There was no wind, and the water was so very still. It was unusual that there were no wildlife sounds; everything was still and quiet. As we glided across the surface, I noticed the trees were reflected perfectly. It gave me an Alice in Wonderland feeling. The trees seemed to flow from right side up to upside down without interruption.

My mind wandered to the story of Jesus walking on the water when Peter called out to Him, "Lord, if it is you, command me to come to you on the water" in Matthew 14. As long as Peter kept his eyes on Jesus, he walked on the water's surface. As soon as he looked away, he began to sink.

The same thing happens when we, as Christians, lose our focus and waiver in our faith. We look away from Jesus, and our walk becomes a little wobbly, our feet a little heavier as we sink into the mire of the world.

Faith is simply believing in something and then committing our lives to it. Here, the something is God and His Son, Jesus. The Bible tells us in Hebrews 11:1, "Now faith is the assurance of things hoped for, the conviction of things not seen."

We all have faith in electricity, so we believe, when we turn on the switch, the light will come on. Electric currents aren't seen, but we do see the results in the glow of the light bulb or the noise of the dishwasher.

Plug into Jesus and, by faith, allow Him to be the life and light giver to your soul. The results will be amazing!

> Father God, open my eyes, not to see the world more clearly, but to see You. Open my eyes to see you working around me and in me. Nothing happens by accident. You orchestrate every day of my life. Allow me to see your hand in the mundane and the fantastic. Help me to trust in what I cannot see, and believe in Your invisible presence. Amen. (ibelieve.net)

Through a Child's Eyes

Once again, God has used me being with my grandchildren as a spiritual lesson. The children are less than two years old, so everything is new and grand and awesome to them. In fact, Amelia has learned that some things have a *wow* factor! She says wow in a whispery voice drawing out the O in the middle of that three-letter word. When Bryson spies a hummingbird, he grins and points and utters something in that special baby language that only he understands. Much to my chagrin, this has called my attention to things I so often take for granted. Amelia and Bryson are seeing the world with brand-new eyes, and all the creation they encounter elicits a *wow* in one way or another. The Lord has pointed out to me that I need to see with a fresh look as well.

There are several passages of scripture that come to mind when thinking of our view of the world and God's creation. The first verses that God took me to were from Psalm 8:1, 3–4: "Lord our Lord, how excellent is Thy name in all the earth! Who hast set thy glory above the heavens. When I consider thy heavens, the work of thy fingers, the moon and the stars, which thou hast ordained; what is man, that thou art mindful of him? And the son of man that thou visitest him?" From Psalm 19:1: "The heavens declare the glory of God; and the firmament sheweth his handiwork." I also think Psalm 24:1 fits the lesson today: "The earth is the Lord's and the fullness thereof: the world, and they that dwell therein."

Wide-eyed wonder; spirit and mind, like a sponge soaking in all the goodness God has to offer; no analysis; no intellectual debate; no personal agendas; just pure faith, pure trust, awe—these are the eyes of the children.

Watching them gives me joy at their joy, excitement with their excitement and in their way. I think they are praising the God who created it all! They each make a joyful noise as they respond and take in each new and exciting thing they encounter daily.

Are you seeing things as I did, with dull, old eyes, or do you see, with the eyes of a child, those things that God has set before us—His creation for us to enjoy, His glory that we see in the sunrise or sunset, the joy of the children discovering their world?

The words of the hymn "Open My Eyes that I May See" by Clara H. Scott are my prayer today. Won't you make it yours too?

> Open my eyes, that I may see
> Glimpses of truth Thou hast for me;
> Place in my hands the wonderful key
> That shall unclasp and set me free.
> Silently now I wait for Thee,
> Ready my God, Thy will to see,
> Open my eyes, illumine me,
> Spirit divine!

Trust Him

Our pond never ceases to be an instrument of God's peace to me. I can look out over the pond at any time and feel His peace drop over me like a velvet cloak, covering me, causing me to trust in Him. Wrapping myself within its folds, it reminds me of the immovable Jehovah God that protects and provides for me as His child.

I am drawn to Psalm 125:1 that tells us "They that trust in the Lord shall be as mount Zion, which cannot be moved, but abideth forever." If we trust in Him, we will abide forever! How do we maintain this trust?—with faith (1 Peter 1:5) and commitment (2 Timothy 1:12). In Jude 24–25, we find the scripture assures and comforts the believer with these words: "Now unto him that is able to keep you from falling, and to present you faultless before the presence of his glory with exceeding joy, To the only wise God our Saviour be glory and majesty, dominion and power, both now and ever. Amen."

If we will put our trust in Christ through faith and commitment to Him, we will be presented righteous before God the Father. When I consider the pond, I see the glory and majesty of God and better understand His dominion and power.

What a day it will be when our trust makes it so that we can see His glory in all its wonder!

> Christ Jesus,
> when darkness surrounds us
> and we feel our weakness and helplessness,
> give us the sense of Your presence,
> Your love, and Your strength.

PEARLS OF GREAT PRICE

Help us to have that perfect trust
in Your protecting love
and strengthening power,
so that nothing may frighten or worry us,
for, living close to You,
we shall see Your hand,
Your purpose, Your will through all things. Amen.

Grace

Baskets and Washboards

Recently, in talking with my cousin, Joyce, she said that God had given her two words for me, words that, upon first thought, have nothing in common, have no scriptural references, so we were both puzzled at what God had revealed to her. I, nevertheless, wrote them down and have been pondering over them since that day. My prayer, as is hers, is that God will make known what His plan is for these words and that I might have open and discerning eyes as I pray for and meditate on both words: baskets and washboards.

Several weeks of thinking on baskets and washboards and what they might have in common or what even might be their place in a devotional, I felt led to jot down some thoughts. What is the purpose of these two words? Moses was saved in a basket, rescued from the basket, and became God's man to lead the children of Israel out of Egypt. Also, baskets were used to bring the firstfruits to God. The basket for the apostle Paul was a way of escape (Acts 9). Naaman, a leper in the king's service, was told by a little slave girl to seek the prophet of God in Israel, and he could be healed. When Naaman went to Elisha, the prophet sent word to Naaman to go and dip himself in the Jordan River seven times. He did this and became clean with skin as new as a child's. Naaman became a believer in the God of Elisha (2 Kings 5).

I'd like to compare the basket in which Moses was sent out into the river to our physical birth. We come into this world with the protection and love of our parents. However, at the same time, we are entering the unknown. We go through life to the point that we confess our sin and accept Jesus as Savior. There you have the rescue from the basket of birth. Although I reference the basket used in bringing the firstfruits as offerings to God, I also think we can visualize bringing in that basket our sins, burdens, and concerns to Him as well. If we will cast it all to Him, our basket's load will be lightened. Also, we are promised a way of escape in 1 Corinthians 10:13: "There hath no temptation taken you but such as is common to man: but God is faithful, who will not suffer you to be tempted above that ye are able; but will with the temptation also make a way of escape, that ye may be able to bear it."

Looking at the story of Naaman, I envision him dipping himself under the water, in and out of the river seven times. Up and down, up and down until he sees that his skin is like new and clean. This is the same action when using a washboard, up and down with the clothing until all stains have been removed. The garment becomes as new. We, after accepting Jesus as our Lord and Savior, are baptized. The Scriptures tell us in 2 Corinthians 5:17, "Therefore if any man be in Christ, he is a new creature: old things are passed away; behold all things are become new." We go into the baptismal waters "dirty" and are raised cleansed by the blood of Christ.

So maybe baskets and washboards do go together! We are rescued from our basket by Christ and cleansed by the washing of our sins in His blood, the blood shed for us on the cross of Calvary!

Our baskets of dirty laundry are cleaned and washed white as snow by the grace of God in the gift of His Son.

Come As You Are

The old, rusty wheelbarrow now sits in an area of my yard that I refer to as my secret garden. It is in a spot off to the side that we have left in a natural state and added some bird feeders and other accessories to pretty it up, so to speak. There is also a bench so that I can sit to watch the birds closely but not so that they are frightened off by my presence. That wheelbarrow has become my favorite addition to my little space.

We were cleaning out the tractor shed when I spied that old thing; it was surrounded by mowers, a boat, and some junk. Covered in dirt and dust, cobwebs and remnants of a nest of some kind, I immediately knew it was what I needed in my special place! Brooks pulled it out for me. As we cleaned it up a bit, he told me he wasn't sure how old it was, and it might have even been used at the sawmill before the family's company went out of business some forty plus years ago.

I have had that wheelbarrow on my mind since that day, thinking about how we are like it. Pushed out of sight or mind, covered with a layer of dust so much so that it would seem that we like that old wheelbarrow aren't much good. *But God!* Just as I saw potential in the old push buggy just as it is, so our heavenly Father sees us, just as we are!

We can never clean up enough or live good enough to be a child of God on our own. He takes us just as we are and changes us to fit His plan for our lives. I have given the old, well used, and somewhat rusty wheelbarrow a new life, a new purpose. When we give our lives to Jesus, we too are given a new life and purpose for His kingdom.

John 6:37 tells us this: "Everyone whom the Father gives to me will come to me, and I won't send away anyone who comes to me."

It is by *grace* we have been *saved* through faith, and this not from ourselves, it is the gift of God. The good news is, Jesus accepts us just as we are.

Matthew McDonald gives an excellent example in this statement: "When Oliver Cromwell had his portrait painted. It looked perfect, without flaw. However, Oliver Cromwell was not happy as it was not a true reflection of his likeness. He had it done again, he said to the artist, 'Paint me warts and all! I want to people take me as I am, to accept me, for being me.'"

When we come to Jesus, He sees us as we are and accepts us, warts and all, our sinful way of life, our tainted past.

We all have a sinful and tainted past, but there is hope! Take a look at this verse in Isaiah: "Come now and let's settle this, says the Lord. Though your sins are like scarlet, they will be white as snow. If they are red as crimson, they will become like wool."

Meditate on the words of the hymn by Charlotte Elliott, "Just as I Am," as we close today.

> Just as I am, thou wilt receive,
> wilt welcome, pardon, cleanse, relieve;
> because thy promise I believe,
> O Lamb of God, I come, I come

Faithful and Unchanging

What a contrast in the weather we've had over the past couple of days! Just yesterday, we had a little snow after having had temperatures in the seventies for the past few weeks. Today, as I was leaving for work, I eyed the beautifully blooming crab apple tree in my yard. Our North Carolina weather can change day to day. In fact, most things in our lives are ever changing. God, however, never changes! He is the same yesterday, today, and tomorrow. What a comforting thought. James 1:17 tells us so, "Every good gift and every perfect gift is from above, and cometh down from the Father of lights with whom is no variableness, neither shadow of turning." He does not vary; He does not turn (change).

We read in Malachi 3:6, "For I am the Lord, I change not; therefore ye sons of Jacob are not consumed."

To further explain this verse, the following excerpt is from bibletools.org: "God's mind is absolutely undivided. In practical application, this means that His sovereignty can never be separated from His love; His grace cannot be separated from his omniscience; His judgment cannot be separated from either His mercy or His wrath. GOD is absolutely constant because His faithful providence cannot be separated from any other of His attributes. God is whole and complete. Under every circumstance, He is never confused or uncertain about what to do. He is always headed in the same direction, which is to complete His purpose" (John Ritenbaugh).

In this world of change, put your trust in an unchanging God. Know that He wants the best for you and that He knows what is best.

Even when we are faithless, He remains faithful, for He cannot deny Himself. This truth is from 2 Timothy 2:13.

In closing think on these words from the hymn "Immortal, Invisible, God Only Wise."

> To all, life Thou givest, to both great and small;
> In all life Thou livest, the true life of all;
> We blossom and flourish as leaves on the tree,
> And wither and perish—but naught changeth
> Thee. (Walter C. Smith)

He Changes Not

This morning, there was a pair of wood ducks on the pond, working the edge nearest my bay window. The male was a little further from the bank, but the female was about as shallow as she could be without beaching herself. Her mate was following a bit behind, as if acting as her guardian while she searched for food. He appeared to be focused on her and waiting patiently as she was foraging. Something seemed to distract her, and I watched as she came right up into the backyard a few feet before turning back to the pond. The male duck didn't change his position or attention.

This picture brought to mind the way we, as Christians, sometimes move along in our own thoughts and actions, even getting distracted and wandering around aimlessly while, Jesus, just like the male duck in our devotion today, stayed the course. His attention to his mate didn't waiver; his position didn't change.

Our relationship with Jesus is very much the same. When the things of this world pull at us and at least for me, manage to get our attention away from the things of God, and we are cruising with our head in the water, so to speak, leaving the straight path for the one that puts distance between us and the Lord. He never alters His watch, care, and attentiveness toward us. When there is a change in our relationship, it is we who have changed.

This truth is found in Hebrews 13:8, "Jesus Christ is the same yesterday, today and forever."

If you find yourself drifting away from God, remember it is not Him that has moved and get back into His Word, recommit your life to Him and step back toward Him, and you will find that He is waiting for you in the very place you left Him.

The final verse of the poem "Our God Changes Not" by M. S. Lowndes sums it all up for us:

> So, even though this world's unstable,
> He's still our solid rock,
> And the only certainty in life,
> For our God changes not.

Indescribable Grace

Carried along on the breeze, I heard the familiar tune of "Amazing Grace" as I sat on the porch one early spring morning. One of my sets of wind chimes is mounted near the porch, and it was a beautiful accompaniment as I was reading my Bible. This particular set is tuned to that great hymn, and it sounded absolutely heavenly. I have several sets of chimes outside. Although they were all singing in the breeze, the "Amazing Grace" ones sounded above all the others.

I have mixed emotions when I hear that song; it is the only song my daddy mentioned wanting sung at his funeral service. He, like a lot of others, loved that song, and it meant something special to him. My daddy was in his late sixties when he was baptized, and he died at age seventy-three. What grace it was that brought him to that decision at such a late age and not too long before he left this earth!

My father worked as a chef most all of his life, which required him to work most Sundays, not to mention every night. It wasn't often that he was able to go to church with my mother and me; in fact, it was after his retirement when he began to go to church regularly, and he attended with us at Crestview. In the fall of 1995, we found out that he had cancer, and there was nothing that could be done to extend his life. He was spiritually ready whenever God called. Without God's gift of grace, that wouldn't have been possible. "For by grace ye are saved through faith: and that not of yourselves, it is the gift of God" (Ephesians 2:8).

Many people spoke to me of the grace he showed while he fought the cancer that invaded his body, but he could only do so because God had given His marvelous grace to him. Even though he had asked for the hymn "Amazing Grace," we felt led to use another one: "Marvelous Grace." The songs carry the same message, and I directly relate the last stanza to my daddy's life.

> Marvelous, infinite, matchless grace,
> Freely bestowed on all who believe!
> All who are longing to see His face,
> Will you this moment His grace receive? (Julia H. Johnston)

God is waiting to bestow this same marvelous, infinite, and matchless grace on you! Will you accept it?

Marvelous Grace

" For the believer, harsh, critical, impatient, and irritated responses to others are always connected to forgetting or denying who we are and what we have been given in Jesus." This is what jumped out at me in one of my devotions this week from Paul David Tripp. Whoa! That's a deep thought and certainly put me to thinking! In this devotion, he was speaking about grace, both having been given grace and giving grace to others. We can't begin to give grace to others without the realization of the grace that has been bestowed on us from Christ.

What exactly is grace? The dictionary defines it several ways, but for our purpose, I've chosen the first entry, which says grace is (1) unmerited divine assistance to humans for their regeneration or sanctification and (2) a virtue coming from God. We, who are His children, have all been recipients of immeasurable grace. John's gospel says it like this: "From his fullness we have all received grace upon grace" (1:16). The *Believer's Bible Commentary* explains it as *abundant grace; God's gracious favor which He showers on His beloved children.*

As Christians, we are expected to recycle that grace to those we come in contact with in our daily lives. Truly, to whom much is given (grace), much is required (grace passed on). I would say, in the past eighteen or so months, I have seen less grace in action. So I go back to the statement from Paul David Tripp and think how many times I have exhibited all of those responses in one situation or another. I forgot about the grace I'd been so freely given! That statement has made me more determined to do my best to share what I have received in Christ to those I encounter on my life's journey.

Let us not forget our gift of grace. In today's terms, let's regift it to others. As it is described in the old hymn, that marvelous, infinite, matchless grace can be passed on only because we have been given it fully and freely.

"We love because God first loved us" (1 John 4:19) could just as easily be saying we extend grace because God first gave us grace.

When we consider our grace has come at the sacrifice of Christ on the cross, we should be anxious to share it with others!

Now is the Time

As I've pondered this devotion, I was drawn back to some notes I'd jotted down with a date of March 6, 2019, about one year from the dreaded pandemic call of March 2020. The Lord kept taking me back to one passage from 2 Corinthians 6:1–2, which is, "Since we work together with him, we are also begging you not to receive the grace of God in vain. He says, I listened to you at the right time, and I helped you on the day of salvation. Look, now is the right time! Look, now is the day of salvation!" I chose to pull this from my Common English Bible because this translation makes the warning sound much more ominous.

Webster's Dictionary gives a definition of in vain as "to no end: without success or result." This is a sobering thought that I might receive God's grace in vain, without success or result. We must share our marvelous message of hope and of the Savior of whom it tells.

In light of all that has happened within the last year and a half, it is imperative that we not ignore that *today* is the day of salvation! Many people are looking for answers, and we, as Christ's followers, have the answer, and that answer is to know Christ.

As Christians, we remain steadfast in that God is in control. Nothing that we see and hear on the news is news to Him. He has looked down through time to the day in which we are living. We have the hope of eternal life because of the grace of our loving God.

Don't take God's grace for granted, and don't hold onto it for yourself. Share it so that your receiving it wasn't in vain.

May this be our prayer as we share Christ with others:

LUCY ALLEN

So they can come before You
And worship You with praise,
To come into Your presence, Lord,
And receive Your saving grace. (M. S. Lowndes)

Standing Firm

Trials and testing—who has not experienced them? From minor to major, we will all have trials and tests in this life; however, we have a promise. In John 16:33, we read this: "In the world you will have distress. But be encouraged! I have conquered the world." I'll go as far to say we're to have joy in our trials. James 1:2 tells us, "Brothers and sisters, think of the various tests you encounter as occasions for joy." Joy?—yes, joy as a supernatural delight in the person and purposes of God.

In the past almost two years, we have had trials, and at times, it has been hard to see that joy. I have needed reminders of how to have joy in the worrisome times. Some days it has been hard to see what Paul wrote to the Romans in Romans 8:28: "We know that God works all things together for good for the ones who love God, for those called according to His purpose." This statement from The Believer's Bible Commentary gives this explanation: "Whatever God permits to come into our lives is designed to conform us to the image of His Son." As I read this morning in my devotional, God is in the here and now, performing His redemptive work on His children! God tied my personal devotion to this devotion He had already planted in my head!

We have a part to play in rising above our trials and tests as well. God does expect us to trust and stand firm in our faith in Him during these times. Some days, there were no answers. I knew He was in control, and we had to put our trust in that fact and just let Him hold it.

Today I can see God's hand in each situation, how He guided and directed, how He put people in places to work things out for good. As long as we are living in this old world, we will have these trials and tests from time to time.

As I close today's devotion with that thought, I pray the following verse from James 1:12 brings you renewed hope and joy in the midst of any trial or test you may be facing:

> Those who stand firm during testing are blessed. They are tried and true. They will receive the life God has promised to those who love Him as their reward.

Throwing Rocks

Our little grandson just loves to throw rocks into the pond. He is just as pleased with a small splash as with a big one. With each rock he picks up, he looks up at me and says "rock," to which I reply yes again and again. A few days ago, since we had a couple of really pleasant afternoons, Bryson and I ventured outside, and sure enough, we ended up sitting in the grass, throwing rocks. The problem was, we had to constantly search for rocks! We gathered up a few small piles along the bank of the pond, and eventually, every last rock was in the water.

Being a rock gatherer all afternoon set me to thinking about how Jesus is our rock. Unlike having to continue searching for and collecting rocks each time we depleted our throwing supply, our rock is everlasting! This truth is found in Isaiah 26:4: "Trust in the Lord forever, for the Lord is a rock for all ages." Once you have placed your trust in Jesus as your rock, it is done. If we rest on the foundation that is Christ, then as we sing in the old hymn, "On Christ the Solid Rock I Stand," His oath, His covenant, His blood support us in the whelming flood!

We don't have to run to and fro, trying to gather up enough Jesus to throw into our days. His death on the cross was a one-time sacrifice. First Peter 3:18 is one of my favorite references to this truth: "Christ himself suffered on account of sins, once for all, the righteous one on behalf of the unrighteous." In addition, once we are saved by grace through faith, we are saved! No question about it. We must confess our sins, but the promise to our confessions is that they are forgiven and forgotten forever.

I don't think I will pick up rocks ever again that I am not reminded of this truth.

Are you standing on that solid rock today? Once you have committed to stand on the rock, you won't need to search anymore. Look back at the verse from Isaiah; He is a rock for all ages!

Hope

An Anchor of Hope

Like an endless loop of film, the image of a ship's anchor kept running through my mind for days. I haven't been on a boat to think about an anchor, and the little anchor for our boat isn't anything but a weight on the end of a rope, so why was I constantly thinking about an anchor? Although the shape of the anchor is curved, I still considered it a likeness to the cross of Christ, and in that light, it also reflects the characteristic we associate with Christ as being our anchor. We find these words in Hebrews 6:19: "Which hope we have as an anchor of the soul, both sure and stedfast, and which entereth into that within the veil."

> In addition to the anchor being a symbol of terrestrial and eternal *hope*, the shape of an anchor simulates the shape of the Cross upon which Jesus died for our sins. In early Christian iconography in the Roman catacombs (c. late 100–400 AD), one often finds on the tombs of the dead Christians an anchor as a symbol of their firm hope in an eternal life with their Savior. (EarlyChurchHistory.org)

That hope, that anchor, is none other than Jesus Christ, and it is He who enters into God's presence before us (behind the veil). In the Old Testament, we know that only the high priests could enter the veil to the mercy seat. Today, that veil has been torn away, and we have a divine High Priest standing in for us. What is the job of an anchor?—to fix or secure in a particular place. Jesus has, by His death on the cross, fixed and secured the believer a spot in the greatest particular place!—a place to spend eternity in worship and service to God with fellow believers.

Anchors hold the ship steady while riding out a storm in the midst of the sea or in calm waters in a safe port. As Christians, we experience both the storms of life and seasons of floating peacefully. In either case, an anchor is a must-have! Without it, we would be tossed to and fro, drifting aimlessly about in life.

> For the Christian, Christ is "the Way, the Truth, the Life" (John 14:6) and the anchor of our soul who fastens and fixates both our hope here on earth and in the world to come. (Sandra Sweeny Silver)

A passage for further study is Ephesians 4:11–16.
Are you fastened to *the* anchor today?

But God

As I was reading my morning devotion, which was about troubles in life, it reminded me of the phrase from Macbeth, "double, double toil and trouble." We have trouble on every hand these days, or so it seems. The line is catchy and certainly fitting for the current world condition.

This thought brings a "but God" point to mind. In 2 Corinthians 4:8–9, we read, "We are experiencing all kinds of trouble, but we aren't crushed. We are confused, but we aren't depressed. We are harassed, but we aren't abandoned. We are knocked down, but we aren't knocked out." A few verses on in this same passage, Paul tells us that these temporary, minor problems are producing an eternal stockpile of glory for us beyond all comparison!

So there is the "but God"! These words change everything! Although those exact words don't appear in our scripture selection today, the idea most assuredly does. There are many "but God" verses in the Bible, and generally, following those sweet words is a promise and a hope for His children, once we were dead in sin, once we were separated from Him, once we were looking at hell... *but God!*

Charles Spurgeon explains it like this: "To be snatched from the devouring fire or saved from fierce disease, just when the turning point has come, and death appears imminent, these are also occasions for crying, 'Saved!' But to be rescued from sin and hell is a greater salvation still and demands a louder joy. We will sing it in life and whisper it in death and chant it throughout eternity—saved by the Lord!"

I had not thought of it before, but as I wrote this devotion, I started to wonder about the first person of the Bible to have had a "but God" moment. In thinking about when one experiences such a moment, most often in trying times that require action from God on our behalf. I discovered that Noah witnessed the first ever *but God*. He was living in days as turbulent, chaotic, and sinful as those we live in today.

Genesis 7 gives us the account of Noah and his family with the animals all entering into the ark and the flood that destroyed all other life on earth. Imagine being in that vessel, tossed about, hearing terrible sounds of the dying outside of the ark. What faith it must have taken to not wonder if God would indeed pull them through. Then we read in Genesis 8:1, "But God remembered Noah, all those alive and with him in the ark."

Around forty-five times these powerful words appear in the Bible. So take heart. Remember that whatever your situation today can be changed. Romans 5:8 reminds us of this truth: "But God shows His love for us, because while we were yet sinners Christ died for us."

But God…

Follow the "Sonlight"

There! Just off the shoulder of the road, we passed the prettiest little sunflower field! On our way to or from somewhere recently, I noticed this happy patch on the roadside. I love sunflowers; they just bring bright, happy thoughts to mind. Did you know that sunflowers follow the sun? Thewonderofscience.com explains it this way: "According to researchers only young sunflowers will follow the Sun. These flowers are following a natural circadian rhythm to receive the most light for photosynthesis."

I know that God placed the circadian rhythm within each flower, so I can go along with the explanation. I also see a correlation between flower, and we Christians are we not to follow the Son? By following in Jesus's footsteps and living a life pleasing to Him, we too will receive the most light for life! Jesus tells us this in John 8:12, "Jesus spoke to the people saying, I am the light of the world. Whoever follows me won't walk in darkness but will have the light of life."

In Jesus is life and light to all who will receive Him. Without this light, we exist in a spiritual darkness, but Christ will lead us out of darkness, and we ourselves will be a light to others. With life and light, we can move boldly through the darkness of this world as a witness for the One who is the source of all light.

Carry your light high, and be a bearer of hope in the night rather than a spreader of fear and shadows. After all, as Christians, we're called to always be ready to give an answer for the hope that is in us. We read in 1 Peter 3:15, "Regard Christ as holy in your hearts.

Whenever anyone asks you to speak of your hope, be ready to defend it."

As children, most, if not all of us, learned the song "This Little Light of Mine," and its message still rings true for us as adults. Even though there are three verses, I would bet, like me, you probably only remember the first verse. Today, in closing this devotion, I would like you to read through the third verse and ponder on it. How will you shine your light?

> Jesus gave it to me,
> I'm gonna let it shine.
> Jesus gave it to me,
> I'm gonna let it shine.
> Jesus gave it to me,
> I'm gonna let it shine,
> let it shine, let it shine, oh let it shine. (Harry Dixon Loes)

Hearts of Life

After three weekends of wintery weather and frigid temperatures, I was more than a little surprised when I caught sight of a flash of red on one of my camellia bushes. There, tucked between the leaves, was not one, or even two, but multiple blooms shyly showing their brilliant red petals centered with bright yellow stamens! I did a little happy dance! I was certain, the freezing weather had done them in, but there they were, as if to say, "you can't keep us down!"

God, as is so often the case, spoke to me through nature in this camellia bush. I had assumed the worst that the blooms weren't coming this time due to the bleak and cold days we'd experienced. Just as that thought registered with me, I realized, that is what occurs in our hearts when we accept Jesus Christ as our Savior. Our hearts bloom after, sometimes years of bleakness and being frigid! Yes, Christ can take our hearts, once dead in trespasses and sin and bring life. Ezekiel 11:19 says this: "I will give them one heart, and I will put a new spirit in them. I will remove the stony hearts and give them hearts of flesh."

It is a heart religion that God desires, and our hearts are beyond repair. Through Christ, a new heart is provided to all who invite Him to live within them, and He, in exchange, offers everlasting life! I love the way Proverbs 4:23 reads in the English Standard Version, so I will use it for today's devotion. It says simply, "Keep your heart with all vigilance, for from it flow the springs of life." There is the promise of the spring of life we obtain by giving our hearts to Jesus.

I don't think you have to be unsaved to have a bleak or frigid heart. I think situations and circumstances can cause us to harden our hearts for a season. If you find yourself in a cold and wintery heart season, make your prayer today from Psalm 51:10: "Create a clean heart for me, God; put a new faithful spirit deep inside me!"

If perhaps you don't know Jesus as your Savior, I would direct you to the Gospel of John. If you feel His wooing, you can whisper a simple prayer, such as this one:

Dear Lord Jesus, I know that I am a sinner, and I ask for Your forgiveness. I believe You died for my sins and rose from the dead. I turn from my sins and invite You to come into my heart and life. I want to trust and follow You as my Lord and Savior. Amen.

Resisting the Attack

As is my habit, I glanced out the bathroom window after I finished moving laundry from the washer to the dryer and spied the bluebird poking its head out of the bluebird box. Thinking that would make a great photo, I slipped out the back door and around the side of the house in hopes of snapping her picture. What was I thinking? As soon as she saw movement in, she ducked! I decided to give her a couple of minutes before giving up and heading back inside to the cool air. While I was standing there, two buzzards caught my attention, circling a few yards from my position. Having seen no more of the bluebird and the thought that those buzzards might be eyeballing something near my front yard sent me over to see if I could see anything that would be of interest to them. Thankfully, I saw nothing!

When buzzards circle, they are checking to see if it is safe, and then they drop down to feast on the remains of some animal. When one buzzard drops down, that is a signal to other buzzards nearby to come and join in the meal. The Lord used those buzzards to give me this devotion! I compare the buzzards to Satan as described in 1 Peter 5:8, "be clear headed. Keep alert. Your accuser, the devil, is on the prowl like a roaring lion, seeking someone to devour." Like the buzzards, Satan circles around in search of someone to attack. I can imagine that many of his demons hang around nearby, waiting for a signal to also dive down into the assault.

What can we do to protect against Satan's attacks? By standing firm in the faith, we can resist him (1 Peter 5:9). We can also look at Hebrews 4:16 for encouragement, which says, "Let us draw near to the throne of favor with confidence so that we can receive mercy and find grace when we need help." There is no better illustration of what this looks like than Jesus Himself. At the beginning of His earthly ministry, He had to resist the devil in the wilderness. Even though Jesus was God in flesh, He resisted Satan by submitting to the will of the Father and quoting Scripture. For us to think that we can resist the devil, any other way is foolish!

Because Christ has already won the victory, we *can* resist the devil! Resisting is a daily spiritual battle. Won't you make this prayer part of your time with the Lord each and every day?

> Lord Jesus, I thank you that you have already won the victory. Because of your death on the Cross, Satan's fate has been sealed. Thank you for equipping and enabling me to resist the devil's attacks. Thank you for your Word that can expose my own sinful desires and refute the lies of the Devil. Help me to stand firm, rooted in the faith, shielded by your armor, and dependent on your grace. Help me to resist the devil today. In the name of the one who crushed the head of the serpent, Amen. (www.crosswalk.com)

The Pot and the Potter

It never ceases to amaze me what God uses to put a thought in my head to use as a devotion. Sometimes the intent is very clear, other times I have to ponder it for a bit and do a little digging before He shows me what I am to write. The scripture that came to mind for this lesson was a very familiar one, but I had to dig deeper to get what I feel is the direction the Lord is taking me.

As I was cleaning up some plants and pots on my patio, this scripture came to me so clearly. I stopped what I was doing to read it for myself. It is 2 Corinthians 4:7: "But we have this treasure in clay pots so that the awesome power belongs to God and doesn't come from us." What exactly was I to get from this verse? I wasn't even cleaning out any clay pots! I highlighted the verse and went back to the patio, running this over and over in my mind.

What I have learned in my deep dig on this verse is that you and I are the clay pots—some translations use earthen vessels—and that treasure that is spoken of is the gospel. I see two thoughts here: (1) Clay pots are fragile, therefore easily broken, and (2) the pots are shaped and molded by the hands of the potter. We know that His strength is made prefect in our weaknesses (2 Corinthians 12:9), and our heavenly Father is the master potter.

We are formed and shaped for the work God has in His plan for us. No matter how fragile or weak we are, if we are living in His will, we have that awesome power of His strength working through us. We must be careful to give the glory and honor to Him for it all. If we were pieces of perfection, without flaws, beautiful, and polished then others would see us and not Christ.

To help us remember who we are, read Psalm 139, focusing on verse 13: "You are the one who created my innermost parts; you knit me together while I was still in my mother's womb." This passage goes on to tell us that God saw us. Even then, His plan was being written for our lives.

In these days of confusion and chaos, sometimes it can be easy to become discouraged and, for a moment, forget whose child we are.

Below is a prayer for when you need a reminder who you belong to and what treasure each of us hold:

> Dear God, there are moments when I forget who I am and the treasure you have given me. In my moments of doubt and weakness, would you remind me that you have chosen me? You have placed within me a treasure that will strengthen me in my greatest weakness. Would you help me remember who it is that you have made me to be…and who it is that lives within me? Help me to live in the power that's been given to me. Amen. (Crosswalk.com)

Water of Hope

Palm Sunday, a beautiful day—but due to the COVID-19 threat, we were at home, so we decided to ride in the pedal boat around our pond as the late afternoon hours lazed by.

Brooks was fishing, and I was just relaxing, enjoying the warm sun and easy breeze, when a dragonfly caught my eye. It was flying low, skimming the surface of the pond, dipping down every few seconds to actually touch the water. My thought, as I watched this dance along the surface, was about how I should be constantly dipping into God's Word, keeping my toes in the living water.

In these days, we find it is our hope in Christ that keeps us centered and confident.

Psalm 119:9–11 says, Wherewithal shall a young man cleanse his way? By taking heed thereto according to thy word. With my whole heart have I sought thee: O let me not wander from thy commandments. Thy word have I hid in my heart that I might not sin against thee.

Healing and hope can be found in the water, the living water, Christ Jesus. Look at Job 14:8–9: "Though the root thereof wax old in the earth, and the stock thereof die in the ground; Yet through the scent of water it will bud, and bring forth boughs like a plant."

Our sins are forgiven, our hearts renewed to holiness, and heaven will be the rest for our souls, providing both healing and hope.

Remember that Christ is also the Word. Hide the Scriptures and the person of Christ in your heart, and dip into the living water daily!

Living a Christian Life

Dare to be Red

A few days ago, while we were out for an afternoon jaunt around our property, I spied a burst of red among several branches of still green leaves. It really grabbed my attention, so I spun the golf cart around for a closer look. There, just on the edge of the woods, was a single branch of red leaves surrounded by leaves of green. I snapped a picture for later use! The more I thought about what I'd seen, the more I was reminded of Paul's admonition in Romans 12:2: "And be not conformed to this world: but be ye transformed by the renewing of your mind, that ye may prove what is that good, and acceptable, and perfect, will of God." This means that we, as Christians, are not to allow the world to squeeze us into a mold of its own.

How then do we prevent being molded by this world in which we live? We must study God's word and think like God thinks. As we experience the direct guidance of God in our lives, we will discover His will is that which is good, acceptable, and perfect.

My encounter with these leaves of red also brought to mind something my mama said to me many times: "If everyone else jumped off a cliff, would you jump too?" In other words, don't be like everyone else. Be different! This is exactly what we are called to be: different! Don't follow what the world offers. We have to be in the world but not *of* the world.

So like my little patch of red amid all the green, dare to be a standout! Dare to be different. Dare to be a Daniel!

>Dare to be a Daniel
>Dare to stand alone
>Dare to have a purpose firm
>Dare to make it known. (P. P. Bliss)

Feasting on Solid Food

Recently, Brooks called me outside to look at the baby bluebirds in their nest in the bluebird box. Just a few weeks before, we had only seen one egg, therefore we were shocked to see four little tiny birds in the box! That day, as he opened the top of the box, all four babies were waiting with mouths wide open for the mama bird to come and feed them. Bluebirds do not regurgitate food for the babies as do some birds. In this family, the daddies supply the mama birds with small, soft insects, which they feed to the hatchlings. While peering into the bird box amazed both by the fact that we had four birds, not just one, and that they were so very tiny to be on a soft-food diet, the following scripture came into my mind: 1 Corinthians 3:2. Paul was referring to immature Christians needing to be spiritually fed by milk, like babies, when he said, "I gave you milk to drink instead of solid food, because you weren't up to it yet."

I like the explanation provided on www.reviveourhearts.com, which says, "The Bible talks about milk and solid food in reference to our spiritual growth. When we first come to faith in Christ, we begin with milk; we begin with the basics of the gospel. As we grow and mature, we start feasting on solid food. We dig deeper into Scripture. We learn more about the doctrines of God. Throughout our life of faith, we continue to eat rich spiritual food." I think this explains the scripture reference very well. As for our baby birds, as they grow, the female will increase the size and toughness of their food. As we grow in our Christian walk, we should be digging deeper into God's Word, thereby increasing the size and toughness of our scriptural diet.

Like babies transitioning to solid food, we have to develop a taste for it. They say it takes at least ten times of trying a new food before you like it. When it comes to feasting on God's Word, we develop the taste and desire for it through practice. The more we read and study, the more God's Word transforms us and the more we realize how much we need it. In Hebrews 5:12–14, we find the following instruction: "Although you should have been teachers by now, you need someone to teach you an introduction to the basics about God's message. You have come to the place where you need milk instead of solid food. Everyone who lives on milk is not used to the word of righteousness, because they are babies. But solid food is for the mature, whose senses are trained by practice to distinguish between good and evil."

There are days that I feel that I have regressed to having to be fed "milk" again. I think this is not unusual because we are, after all, in our hearts, sinful creatures. We can, though, ask for forgiveness and delve back into the Word, returning to solid food.

If you find yourself as I do sometimes, I encourage you to make this prayer part of your daily quiet time prayers:

Sovereign God, Your word calls us to come to Christ like little children, dependent upon His grace. We are not to remain as children but to grow and mature in the faith, moving from milk to solid food. May we feast on Your Word, savor its taste, and hunger for it all our days.

In the name of Your Son, Jesus, amen.

Look to the Light

No sooner than I'd said that we hadn't seen any snakes this summer, one slithered out of the wood line as my daughter, grandson, and I rode by in the golf cart! We were unprepared to take on a snake. So as most women would, we began yelling for my husband as I turned the cart around and headed for the house! He was also unprepared, barefoot, and no weapon with which to take on this creepy crawler. I guess the lights from the golf cart hypnotized the snake, for he hardly moved once I got him in my lights. My husband found a large stick and was then able to kill the snake. It was a copperhead, about twelve inches in length.

I knew right away there would be a lesson from this encounter, and in fact, I believe this story offers two spiritual lessons. The first is how easily and quickly sin can slip in, just like this snake. Quietly and stealthily, he slid out of the cover of the woods, right into our lives! Real and threatening, as Brooks approached him, he took on striking posture—so like Satan! We go on living life, and all of a sudden, that great deceiver, liar, and destroyer shows up. Here, we look to 1 Peter 5:8 for how to be prepared: "Be sober, be vigilant; because your adversary the devil, as a roaring lion, walketh about, seeking whom he may devour."

Secondly, what brought that serpent under compliance but light…yes, *light*! Christ, the light of the world, brings Satan under subjection. This truth is found in Matthew 28:18 where Jesus tells us, "All power is given unto me in heaven and in earth." Jesus's authority overrules Satan's authority, and he can have no hold on us, who are believers and followers of Christ.

We Christians must read our Bibles and spend time in prayer to remain sober and vigilant and trust that Jesus has all power and authority in heaven and earth.

Be aware and watchful day-to-day, and be sure your *light* is on and bright!

Sifted and Worthy

The sand fell like sugar through the sifter, leaving tiny pebbly residue behind as I shook the plastic sandbox toy. As the fine silvery sand dropped free and landed once again into the children's sandbox, I realized the similarity I was seeing to biblical sifting: dividing the wheat and tares, the separating of things to be discarded from things kept.

There are several Scriptures that reference being sifted. Look at Amos 9:9: "Look, I am giving orders, and I will shake the house of Israel among all the nations as one sifts dirt with a screen, but no pebble will fall to the ground." In this passage, God promised to save a remnant, as pebbles in a sieve, not the smallest pebble would fall to the ground. Any found worthy by God Almighty would be spared.

The question now is, how are we found worthy? We read the answer in Luke's gospel, 21:36: "Watch ye therefore, and pray always, that ye may be accounted worthy to escape all these things that shall come to pass, and to stand before the Son of man." In the previous verses, Luke was writing Jesus's warnings, things to watch for in expectation of His return.

Paul tells us in Colossians 1:10 as part of his prayer, "That ye might walk worthy of the Lord unto all pleasing, being fruitful in every good work, and increasing in the knowledge of God." To be worthy, we, as Christians, must be fruitful and increase our knowledge of God and His word.

LUCY ALLEN

Back to that toy sifter, I pray that I might be found worthy and remain as those little pebbles did, held safe by the One who sifts us.

Sift me, Lord
That I may stay
Ever worthy, day by day.

Love

Are You a Scorekeeper?

I have a confession to make. While I was working in the yard recently, I found myself grumbling about why some tasks had not already been taken care of. My attitude morphed into a muttering about different projects that were yet undone. I began to feel bitter and unsympathetic toward my husband, whose job, I felt, was to accomplish these things. Make a list of those items still to complete, that's what I would do! I'd keep account of all the things I wanted him to finish, and I'd point them out of course!

Apply the brakes right here! Before I could get inside, let alone create the "list," God stopped me in my tracks with this nugget from 1 Corinthians 13: the *love* chapter. The last part of verse 5 reads like this: "(love) it doesn't keep a record of complaints." Scratch that list and begin a different one was what God was telling me.

To share a few of the things on the new list: Brooks (1) cooks breakfast and cleans up most every morning; (2) he pitches in when I need babysitting help; (3) he handles the finances and such. I could name a few more, but this was enough to get me to thinking, *So what if he didn't blow the leaves away when I first asked.*

Lesson learned, you might say, but most likely, I will need to be reminded again. According to Jeremiah 17:9, "The heart is deceitful above all things, and desperately wicked: who can know it?" God knows my heart and will convict and correct. My intentions are good, but not being perfect, I will fail. I am thankful that I serve the One who is perfect and have the promise of forgiveness.

This quote from Pastor Randy Smith puts this into modern thoughts: "The flesh loves to store the ways others wrong us. It loves to dwell on these wrongs and exaggerate them exponentially. And it longs for the opportunity when they can be fired back at the one who wronged us as ammunition to get even or execute revenge." True. And to see what our ammunition to fight this is, reflect on 1 John 4:16: "We have known and have believed the love that God has for us. God is love, and those who remain in love remain in God and God remains in them."

In closing for your meditation:

Love is Patient

Love is patient, love is kind.
It does not envy, it does not boast,
it is not proud.
It is not rude, it is not self-seeking,
it is not easily angered,
it keeps no record of wrongs.
Love does not delight in evil
but rejoices with the truth.
It always protects, always trusts,
always hopes, always perseveres.
Love never fails. (1 Corinthians 13:4–8)

As God's Hands

If you look at just the right angle, you can see the handprints of the grandchildren on my glass doors. How precious are those tiny hands! I know I should get the Windex and clean my doors, but I hesitate to remove the tangible evidence that they have been here. As I was contemplating how to form this into a devotion, the Lord led me to this verse in the Scriptures: "Look, on my palms I've inscribed you; your walls are continually before me" (Isaiah 49:16). We are marked by God's handprints from head to toe. He has identified us with Himself. His hands molded each one of us and made us into who we are. His hands are so enormous that He has engraved everyone into His palm. Like a life-size dye cast, He has shaped our soul.

We desperately need His tender touch. You and I need the hand of God to reshape us daily into His original design and purpose. Just as the children have left their handprints for me to see and anyone else who comes into my house before I clean them off, others will see God's handprint on us by the way we live our lives—tangible evidence of God within us.

Every day, you meet people who are recipients of your handprints. Just as the hands of your heavenly Father mark you, so you mark others. This quote by Boyd Bailey says it perfectly, "Handle others as your heavenly Father handles you." That's a heavy thought to consider, isn't it? I am afraid that I have failed miserably at doing just that.

How are we, as Christians, able to handle others as God the Father handles us?—only by taking the nail-scarred hand of Jesus and learning of God's love. Christ Himself suffered on account of sins, *once* for all, the righteous one on behalf of the unrighteous. He did this in order to bring you into the presence of God (1 Peter 3:18) *(emphasis mine)*. Only by knowing how much God loves us can we then be His hand to others.

The closing thought today is a portion of a beautiful prayer that Mother Theresa prayed daily. May we also make it part of our prayers every day.

> Shine through me, and be so in me that everyone I come
> in contact with may feel Your presence in my soul.

On Business for Our King

Ants, one of God's most industrious creations, are fascinating insects. It seems they have attracted the attention of both my grandchildren. Amelia and Bryson however hold different opinions about the ants. When we visited Amelia and her parents most recently, I made the comment to her not to step on an anthill. Well she took this literally, and the remainder of our visit, anytime we were outside, she would not walk on the dirt. Rather she held up her little hands to be carried. Any attempt to put her down resulted in her clinging on like a little spider monkey! Bryson, on the other hand, has really taken an interest in ants. He will leave whatever he is doing to watch them. He wants to touch them and, yes, sometimes step on them. Between the two of them, I've seen plenty of ants rushing about on business for their queen.

These busy ants made me think about being busy and working for Jesus! The ants are constantly on the move from bringing in food to caring for the eggs laid by the queen. Ants are social insects, and a community can have thousands living in it. All this activity seems like chaos!

We have a King. Do we work as hard for Him? Colossians 3:23–24 says this: "Whatever you do, do it from the heart for the Lord and not for people. You know that you will receive an inheritance as a reward. You serve the Lord Christ."

What work are we to do? Remember that it is by grace though faith and not of works that we have salvation (Ephesians 2:8). Works that are fruit borne out of the reception of this grace may consist of attending worship services, praying regularly, studying Scripture, giving generously and cheerfully, going on mission trips, caring for the poor, loving our neighbors, and most importantly, telling others about this grace we ourselves have been given.

God is not asking that we become so busy that we get focused on how much we can do in the amount of time we have, rather we are to make Him first and honor Him in all that we do.

Will you join me in this simple prayer?

> Use my hands, Lord. Help me to serve. By my actions, may I point to Thee. Your gift was the grace I did not deserve. My prayer, that these faith works, will be a key by which others will come into Your kingdom for all eternity. Amen.

Strand of Love

Late afternoon on the patio, as we were enjoying a few relaxing minutes in a slow-moving swing, my eyes caught the glimmer of what shone like a gossamer thread from the table umbrella to the arm of the chair pushed up to that table. It moved gently in the warm breeze, and I marveled at the strength of that strand of a silken spider's web. I was reminded of how strong our Father's love is for His children.

Let's think about that web. The spider's silk can be stretched two to four times its strength and not break! It is known to be five times stronger than a rod of steel the same diameter! That little silvery strand is just amazing!

This put me to thinking about the strength of the thread between us and our heavenly Father. If that simple spider web is so hard to break, how much more is that strand of love that binds us to Christ? We can find the answer in Romans 8:35, 39: "Who shall separate us from the love of Christ? Shall tribulation, or distress, or persecution, or famine, or nakedness, or peril, or sword? Nor height, nor depth, or any other creature, shall be able to separate us from the love of God which is in Christ Jesus our Lord."

What a promise!

Let us remember how strong that love is each time we see a spider web and that, in short, there is nothing that can separate us from God's love.

The Cardinal's Reminder

A flash of red! Did I imagine it? Cleaning in the bathroom, I had opened the plantation shutters on the window that faced out into the front yard when my eye caught a blur of red. I eased a little closer and peered out. Right there, nearly in my face, was a fat, bright red cardinal perched on a limb in the camellia bush. I stood still in amazement, and he sat for several seconds, giving me a good close-up look. Nothing brightens my day like a beautiful cardinal. They are just cheerful birds, and red happens to be my favorite color.

I know many people consider them bearers of heavenly messages, so this sighting prompted me to do a little research on cardinals in the Scriptures. In Latin, *cardo* means hinge; this brought a thought to me. Isn't Jesus like a hinge, allowing us access to our heavenly Father? *Webster's Dictionary* defines the word hinge as a verb—meaning, to attach or join. Oh boy, through Christ, we are joined to God the Father!

I also found references to the red of the cardinal compared to the red blood of Christ, both examples of everlasting vitality. By Jesus's death on the cross, we have that access through His blood. John 3:16 tells us, "For God so loved the world, that he gave his only begotten Son, that whosoever believeth in him should not perish, but have everlasting life." Vitality is life, and here we have that promise of everlasting vitality.

For me, vitality indicates joy as well. A person with joy in their heart most often lives a life of vitality. So in thinking of everlasting vitality (joy), I go to Psalm 16:11, which says, "Thou wilt shew me the path of life: in thy presence is fullness of joy; at thy right hand there are pleasures for evermore."

Wow! That just ties this thought together for me!

The next time you spot a cardinal, remember, joy and everlasting vitality are given to us by our Father who loves us so much!

Mercy

A Confident Approach

You may have read my earlier devotion about my grandson and his rock throwing. If not, I'll just say this: That boy loves to pick up rocks and throw them into the pond. I think he would pass up a cookie to be able to stay outside to continue throwing his rocks! A recent afternoon found us once again at the pond's edge with a little pile of rocks. After already replenishing this pile a few times, when Bryson next indicated he needed to go in search of more rocks, my response was, "Nope, not now." *Boom!* It hit me immediately…my heavenly Father never tells me that!

Through Jesus Christ, we have total access to the very throne room of God. He never turns His children away. Look at Jeremiah 29:12–13: "When you call me and come and pray to me, I will listen to you. When you search for me, yes, search for me with all your heart, you will find me." There are no "come back later(s)" from Him. In fact, He desires that we come to Him in prayer and lay bare all of our burdens before His feet (1 Peter 5:7). Sometimes I have felt that, surely, I'd dug a trench in front of the throne, yet God continued to meet me there.

God wants us to come to Him in confidence and accordance to His will. We find this truth in 1 John 5:14: "This is the confidence that we have in our relationship with God: If we ask for anything in agreement with his will, he listens to us." In addition, Hebrews 4:16 speaks of this confidence as well: "Finally, let's draw near to the throne of favor with confidence so that we can receive mercy and find grace when we need help." Actually, the word confidence is mentioned 168 times in the Bible, and there are about 25 verses that talk about confidence in God.

Webster's Dictionary has several definitions for the word *confidence*. For this purpose, I picked out these two: (1) the quality or state of being certain and (2) a relation of trust or intimacy. According to the Scriptures we've read, we should approach God in prayer in a state of being certain, of who He is, and that He will hear us. The second definition makes it all click for me as we must first have that trusting and intimate relationship.

Don't be afraid to approach God. Instead, approach Him with confidence, knowing that even though we cannot do this in our own strength, we can do it through Jesus, our great High Priest.

The perfect verse for closing this devotion was penned by John Newton:

> Approach, my soul, the mercy seat,
> Where Jesus answers prayer;
> There humbly fall before his feet,
> For none can perish there.

Clean and Unspotted

Every spring, the pond is bathed in pollen; but I am inclined to think, this year has been the worst. The last few weeks, there has been a thick yellow dust lying on top of the water. It moves with the direction of the winds. Some days it is more toward the left, then others it's mostly to the right side. As I look out today on the pond, I am thinking of how that nasty stuff hides the true beauty of the pond.

This thought brings to mind how our true beauty as children of God is disguised by the "*pollen*" of the world on us. When we spend too much time in the things of this world, it is hard for others to see Christ in us. God is always able to see our hearts. Even when we've slipped off the path, He loves us and is just waiting for our whispered prayer of repentance. It's those we encounter daily on this plane that will have difficulty in seeing that we are in fact Christians.

In James 1:27, we read, "Pure religion and undefiled before God and the Father is this, To Visit the fatherless and widows in their affliction, *and to keep himself unspotted from the world.*" My focus here is the last portion of the verse. According to a quote from *Bibleref.com*, the reference to the world is explained as such: "To be unstained by the world means that we refuse to be driven by our own appetites and desires and selfish goals. It means not compromising with a system that hates God."

How, you may wonder, can we be in the world and not be a part of it?—by spending time in God's Word in prayer and in fellowship with people of like faith. We are not a perfect people, but we are a people saved by a perfect God!

If you realize you've become polluted by your time in worldly things, remember, God knows our frame (Psalm 103:14). All we need to do is prayerfully ask Him to forgive us.

Rise up, shake that "pollen" from yourself, and walk uprightly in the narrow gate that leads to life (Matthew 7:13)!

Favor and Freon

It is mid-June and it's ninety-nine degrees outside! My husband asked me to drive his car the next few days and get the annual inspection done so that the license tag can be purchased for the vehicle. I agreed but with a not so cheerful spirit. You see, the car's air conditioning has not been working. My husband is much more tolerant of that fact than I am, even though he drives approximately thirty-five miles to and from work each day. He just puts all four windows down and opens his sunroof in the evenings for the drive home. I've suggested to him several times that he should go ahead and get this fixed as he doesn't need to drive around in this heat. His response is always, "aw, it's not so bad."

We have a little motto that we use quite often in or about different situations, and it is, "the Lord's favor." We don't account it to luck, coincidence, or karma; it truly is the Lord's favor being poured out for us. Well my husband had a little of that favor this week, having decided that he'd at least get some Freon for the air conditioner, which would temporarily provide some cooler air. He made a stop at the local auto parts store. He was really thinking of me and wanting to ensure that I would be comfortable driving his car. He found that the price of the Freon was a bit steep. While he was mulling this over, a gentleman nearby quietly told him that the Freon could be found at the Aldi grocery store for about half the price in the auto parts store. Thanking him, my better half hopped into his very warm car and drove over to Aldi, purchased several cans of Freon, and came home grinning ear to ear over his favor from the Lord.

After dinner, as he was filling the air conditioner with the Freon, I was reminded of the following scripture from 1 Thessalonians 5:18 that says, "In every thing give thanks: for it is the will of God in Christ Jesus concerning you." I am giving thanks, even for Freon!

Our heavenly Father is concerned with your every need. Too often, we forget that He wants us to come to Him with even the most trivial of requests.

> O give thanks unto the Lord, for He is good:
> For His mercy endureth for ever. (Psalm 107:1)

From Death to Life

It was cold and gray, so the pond looked bleak in the light of the midwinter afternoon. I studied the plant life that circled the pond's edge; it was ragged, tired, and dead in its appearance. It reminded me of how I must have seemed to God before I knew Jesus as my Savior, before I had been forgiven and made righteous in His sight—righteous, only through the blood of Jesus.

I knew this vegetation would soon begin to show forth the tiniest signs of life. Bit by bit, as the weather warms toward spring, shoots and sprigs will become visible among that which seems dead. How much this is like the transforming that occurs once we accept Jesus. At the very moment, we utter the words "come into my heart, Lord Jesus," our lives are immediately transformed!

What an amazing love! That in our deadness, Jesus comes into our hearts and washes them with His shed blood so that, when our heavenly Father looks upon us, He sees us dressed in robes of white, clean and pure. We find this truth in Ephesians 2:4–5: "But God, who is rich in mercy, for his great love wherewith he loved us, Even when we were dead in sins, hath quickened us together with Christ, (by grace are ye saved;)."

Today can be the day your life is changed by God's great love. If you want life to replace the barren, desolate turf of your heart, I invite you to whisper this simple prayer and, by grace, receive salvation.

> Dear Lord Jesus, thank you for dying on the cross for my sin. Please forgive me. Come into my life. I receive You as my Lord and Savior. Help me to live for you the rest of this life. In the name of Jesus, I pray. Amen.

Grip Before You Slip

You've stepped onto the bank of a pond or lake, and before you know it, your foot has slipped, and you've ended up a little bit wet or muddy. I'm sure this has happened to most of us, if not by the water, then perhaps on a hike in the mountains. Your heart skips a beat as you're surely going to roll down the mountain, right? Here at the pond, it's happened to me on several occasions! Brooks has been known to not just have his foot slip but also the mower! What a helpless feeling when your foot slips out from under you no matter where you are.

We simply recover and regain control and proceed on, but what about when that slip is a spiritual one? How is control recovered? Psalm 94:18–19 tells us, "Whenever I feel my foot slipping, your faithful love steadies me, Lord. When my anxieties multiply, your comforting calms me down." I love the way the King James reads, but for this devotion, I feel the Common English version makes the message so clear. Before we're aware of the slip, God has already reached out His right hand to steady us; He calms us in our anxiety. What a comforting thought. What a promise for us as we live each and every day for Him.

Walking with Christ makes us sure-footed; but when the occasional slip happens, reach out for God's hand, for it is there waiting for you to grab hold. Another verse to remember is Psalm 63:8: "My whole being clings to you; your strong hand upholds me."

Grasp and cling to His hand, and remember that He is the one who strengthens, loves, and carries us. Because He is a faithful God, we can always count on the power of His hand.

To the one who is able to protect you from falling, and to present you blameless and rejoicing before his glorious presence, to the only God our savior, through Jesus Christ our Lord, belong glory, majesty, power and authority, before all time, now and forever, Amen. (Jude 24–25)

Splinter of Sin

Recently, our Sunday school teacher made a statement that caught my attention and stuck with me. The discussion was on the person of Jesus, both His humanity and the divine nature He possessed. Jesus was sin-free, and being that we were created in God's image, we too would have been sin-free. This makes sin a foreign object within us. With Adam and Eve's disobedience in the garden, sin came in lodging itself deep within our beings. Left there unconfessed, it will fester like a splinter in the finger that isn't removed. "So, in the same way that sin entered the world through one person, and death came through sin, so death spread to all human beings with the result that all sinned" (Romans 5:12 CEB). This was something I had not thought about, the fact that sin was not in God's original plan for man. However, God knew the turn Adam and Eve would take. From that moment on, sin would have to be dealt with. Once the Lord put this comparison in my mind, I knew it would be my next devotion!

Sin is a foreign object. Left alone, its infection grows and grows within us, much like that splinter we've probably all had at one time or another. Consider this analogy: "Imagine standing by a south window on a cold winter day. The air is frigid, but the sun is shining through the window. It begins to warm you, and you bask in its glow. Then you pull the drape closed. Instantly, the warmth stops. Is it because the sun has stopped shining? No, it is because something has come between you and the sun. The moment you open the drape, the sun can warm you again. But it is up to you. The barrier is inside the house, not outside" (www.gotquestions.org).

Remember back in the first paragraph, sin had to be dealt with after that fateful day in the garden. Many sacrifices later, God sent His Son, Jesus, to take care of all of our sin. That great and terrible day that Jesus died did it all! Sin had been handled; death had been cancelled! There is, though, something required of us: confessing our sin(s). We have received a merciful promise from our heavenly Father that "if we confess our sins, he is faithful and just to forgive us our sins and cleanse us from everything we've done wrong" (1 John 1:9).

God so loved us that He has provided us with a solution to the sin problem! I love this verse from Ephesians 1. Verse 7–8 says, "We have been ransomed through his Son's blood, and we have forgiveness for our failures based on his overflowing grace which he poured over us with wisdom and understanding." Hallelujah!

If there is something festering in your heart that you need forgiveness for, don't hesitate! Kneel before Jesus. Confess and repent, and you will receive that overflowing grace poured upon you.

> Fall on your knees—confess! For that is what is best.
> As far as east is from the west,
> Your sins He will fling
> And pardon it shall bring.
> Don't delay, Confess today!

The Dark Well

There is an old abandoned well out in the field on our property. My husband pointed it out to me one afternoon while we were out on our golf cart. Actually, he did more than point it out; he stopped the golf cart and went over to investigate. I was more than a little skeptical about peering down into the deep blackness of that hole. It is covered in an attempt to keep anyone from falling in. Just the thought of that possibility gave me goosebumps. What an awful place to find yourself if you survived the fall in that deep, dark, and damp hole, out of sight of anyone and probably out of calling distance as well. Would we not think all was lost? There would be no rescuer coming to our aid, which would mean that there, in that hole, far from any hope of rescue we would perish.

How often have we found ourselves in that hole emotionally, financially, or even spiritually? That intangible hole can be just as dark and deep as the actual well in the field. There is a difference in that while no one may be able to reach into the real hole and pull us out, God can reach into the hole in our life and pull us up! There is no place we can find ourselves that God cannot hear our call and reach in to lift us up. This promise is in Isaiah 59:1: "Behold, the Lord's hand is not shortened, that it cannot save; neither is his ear heavy, that it cannot hear."

There is no place too dark as we find in John 1:5: "And the light shineth in darkness; and the darkness comprehended it not." When you are in a room that is blanketed in total darkness, and a candle is lit, the darkness will not overtake the light but rather the light dispels the darkness. If there are dark places in your life today, turn to the light of the world—Jesus. As He begins His work in your life, the light of Christ will become bigger and bigger, and the darkness will recede.

Once we are redeemed and become the children of the King, we are to walk in the light of God's word so that we ourselves may be that light to someone else. Take a look at Ephesians 5:8: "For ye were sometimes darkness, but now are ye light in the Lord: walk as children of light."

Remember, there is no place God cannot reach or hear you. If you find yourself in a deep, damp well of darkness you need only to cry out for Him.

Peace

Can You Hear?

Was I listening? Oh, yes, I was hearing the sounds coming from the landfill as they filtered through the woods, the loggers cutting timber across the road, and lots of chirps and whistles from the many birds in close vicinity to my location on the back porch. I was out there to have some quiet time for my devotions and Bible reading! Ha!

The scripture selection was Psalm 95, which begins as a joyful worship psalm. However, in verse 7, the writer threw me a curve. The end of this verse says, "If only you would listen to His voice right now!" I was jolted into realization that, through all the noise of the world, sometimes I missed the still, small voice of God whispering to me. I like the way this is described in the *Believer's Bible Commentary*. William MacDonald says that "it is the longing, eloquent sighing of the Holy Spirit."

This took me back to when I was a child, and my mama, being frustrated with me, would tell me to please listen to what she had to say. I have done the same with my children on those trying days of childhood when you let out that long, exasperating sigh and those same words, if only you would listen!

So is it the actual noises that drown out the voice of God? No, the machines can't drown it out, nor can the birds. The "noise" is all the chaos, confusion, spirit of deception, and envy that speak so loudly it shifts our attention to itself and off of our Lord. No matter how briefly we miss the opportunity to hear that voice that comes so often as a quiet thought, a whisper of an idea, or a gentle nudge.

How do we turn off those distractions? Our answer is in James 4:8: "Come near to God, and he will come near to you. Wash your hands, you sinners. Purify your hearts, you double-minded." Another truth is found in 1 Kings 19:11–12, where God tells Elijah to go out and stand at the mountain before the Lord. Elijah stood in a wind, earthquake, and fire, but the Lord wasn't in any of them. The end of this passage ends by saying, "After the fire, there was a sound. Thin. Quiet."

God came to Elijah in a gentle whisper. I learned while composing this devotion that the Hebrew for "gentle whisper" is *Kol D'mama Daka*, which is to say, the sound of thin silence. That is where God meets us…in the gentle whisper, the thin silence. If our hearts are still and silent, we will be able to hear Him there.

I love this simple prayer and encourage you to use it if you too are having a hard time listening for and hearing God's voice.

> Dear God, help us draw near to You. We know whatever story You've written for our lives is beautiful—because it's from You. Help us quiet the voices of the world so we may enter into the thin silence, to hear Your gentle whisper and be filled with Your peace in our hearts today. In Jesus' Name, Amen. (Proverbs31.org)

Do Not Fear

My devotions usually reflect a lesson I've learned from nature, and God has used many aspects of His creation to inspire my mind. Today's devotion is not nature related, but I did sense God's direction nonetheless.

As I was reading my Bible and having my prayer time, I was directed to Proverbs 16:2 for the daily scripture selection. As I often do, I read on past that one verse to verse 4 which is, "The Lord made everything for a purpose, even the wicked for an evil day." *Bam!* I had to reread that!—exactly on target with the message Pastor Robby shared on Revelation 13. We are living in evil days certainly, and I know that God's plan from eternity has not changed, and He is not surprised by these days in which we are living. This passage is so plain spoken, it really hit home with me.

The next verse states, *"The Lord detests all who are arrogant; they surely won't go unpunished."* The *Believer's Bible Commentary* explains it like this: There is a result for every cause, a reward or punishment for every act. Evil doers will not escape God's punishment; there is a day for the wicked just as there is a day for believers in heaven!

Do not be discouraged; do not be dismayed; and do not be fearful! Matthew 10:26 says, "Therefore, don't be afraid of those people because nothing is hidden that won't be revealed, and nothing secret that won't be brought out into the open."

We must, by faith and grace, trust our Lord's plan of the ages and not fret. Through prayer and Bible study, we can have the peace that passes all understanding about our world and these days we are living in.

I have a copy of a prayer by an anonymous author that perfectly ends this devotion today. Would you pray it with me?

Renew Your church and this world in ways only You could have foreseen and engineered. In You, O Lord, we place our trust. For You, O Lord, we wait in hope. Thanks be to God. Amen.

In His Shadow

During the heat of the July afternoon, with thunder clouds building in the distance, I was sitting out back on the screened porch, when out of the corner of my eye, I saw two large birds soaring high over the treetops. My attention didn't linger more than a few seconds. However, in a minute or two on the opposite bank of the pond, two large, dark shadows passed overhead. I immediately thought of Psalm 91:1, which says, "Whoever dwells in the shelter of the Most High will rest in the shadow of the Almighty."

What does it mean, to rest in the shadow of the Almighty? Let's look first at the word *rest*. *Webster* defines it as relaxation, to ease up/off, leisure, or to slow down. If you are resting, then I imagine a time of quietness, sitting in your favorite chair, perhaps with a cup of tea, working at nothing, and no worries. There is another definition that caught my eye: rest meaning a support. Does God not support us with His mighty hand? So in light of all this, I think I can reduce the thought to simply casting your burdens upon Him, for He cares for you. We find this truth in Psalm 55:22 and 1 Peter 5:7. This will allow rest for the believer as well as allowing the knowledge that we are held up and held close by God, our heavenly Father.

Now consider the shadow—in particular, the shadow of God. Take a look at Isaiah 51:16: "I have put My words in your mouth and have covered you with the shadow of My hand," or Psalm 36:7: "How precious is Your lovingkindness, O God! And the children of men take refuge in the shadow of Your wings." This shadow, spiritual and supernatural, is portrayed here as a refuge, a protection against something. What a beautiful picture! There are many more references to God's shadow providing protection and refuge in the Bible.

I pray you know that place of quiet rest in the shadow of the Almighty!

The Gift of Life

Friday, June 24, 2022, a significant date for us as Bible-believing Christians! The nearly fifty-year ruling of Roe vs. Wade was overturned by the United States Supreme Court by a count of 6–3! Roe v. Wade, 410 US 113, was a landmark decision of the US Supreme Court in which the court ruled that the constitution of the United States generally protects a pregnant woman's liberty to choose to have an abortion. As a Christian, I am pro-life and do not understand how anyone can say an unborn baby is not a person. Even my great niece recognizes that there are conflicting laws and rules involved. In a conversation with her recently, she made a profound statement (profound for a thirteen-year-old) in that she called attention to the fact that, as a nation, it has been okay to kill the unborn; but if a murder of a pregnant woman results in the death of her unborn child, then that carries two counts of murder, not just one.

The very familiar scripture from Psalm 139:13–16 says, "You are the one who created my innermost parts; you knit me together while I was still in my mother's womb. I give thanks to you that I was marvelously set apart. Your works are wonderful—I know that very well. My bones weren't hidden from you when I was being put together in a secret place, when I was being woven together in the deep parts of the earth. Your eyes saw my embryo, and on your scroll every day was written that was being formed for me, before any one of them had yet happened." I am sure, some of you have had the blessing of seeing your child or grandchild by way of a high-tech ultrasound so you know the feeling of seeing long before you hear it, their tiny precious heart beating at just a few weeks into the pregnancy. Further along, you hear that steady thump-thump of the heart, and brain activity is detected. Tiny fingers and toes are present, and I could go on and on. The point here is that, from day one, this is a living soul to be treasured and protected. In the case of my grandson, his parents saw him as a five-day-old embryo! Our God's creation of human life is…well the only word I can use to express what I am trying to convey is *awesome*. Even this word doesn't do justice to His power and creation process.

God, right off the bat, lets us know that it was He who created mankind. Genesis 1:27 says, "God created humanity in God's own image, in the divine image God created them, male and female God created them." Job, in the midst of all his trials, recognized this truth. He said in Job 31:15, "Didn't the one who made me in the belly make them; didn't the same one fashion us in the womb?"

Praise the Lord that this ruling has finally been overturned. May God forgive us for the years that the voices of His people were silent on this matter. I pray and thank Him today for those justices who did not back down in their convictions and ask that He protects them from the malice and violence that is so prevalent in today's world.

Would you join me in this prayer for life today?

> Father and maker of all, you adorn all creation with splendor and beauty, and fashion human lives in your image and likeness. Awaken in every heart reverence for the work of your hands, and renew among your people a readiness to nurture and sustain your precious gift of life. Grant this through our Lord Jesus Christ, your Son, who lives and reigns with you in the unity of the Holy Spirit, God forever and ever. Amen. (www.usccb.org)

Who Am I?

Following a recent brush with what could have turned into an identity theft situation, Brooks and I had to take steps to protect our personal information. It was not what we had planned to do that afternoon! Scams are everywhere. Even when you think you would never be that gullible, well, then it happens to you. I cannot imagine how many people get hit every day by scammers. After placing some fraud alerts and other safety measures, we feel pretty secure that our information is as safe as it can be. It is mind-blowing how easily somebody can steal your life, taking your identity away from you.

Afterward, contemplating this scary event, I remembered that there is a sure hiding place, a cliff of protection, and hands that hold us so that nothing and nobody can steal us away. That place and those hands are none other than Jesus! Romans 8:38–39 gives us proof of that promise: "I'm convinced that nothing can separate us from God's love in Christ Jesus our Lord: not death or life, not angels or rulers, not present things or future things, not powers or height or depth, or any other thing that is created." My identity is safe in Jesus! Once I gave my life to Him, nothing and no one can separate me from Jesus. What a comforting thought.

In the gospel of John chapter 10, Jesus refers to Himself as the good shepherd before going on in verses 27–29 to say, "My sheep listen to my voice. I know them and they follow me. I give them eternal life. They will never die, and no one will snatch them from my hand. My Father, who has given them to me, is greater than all, and no one is able to snatch them from my Father's hand." Here again is the promise that we cannot be moved once we belong to Jesus. Hallelujah!

Yes, having someone steal your identity and make their way into your bank accounts and credit cards or borrow money as you can wreak havoc in your life, but far worse is to never have identified yourself with Christ.

It is a shame that there are people who do this sort of thing, but the Bible tells us, man's heart is wicked in Jeremiah 17:9, and we read in Proverbs 6:14, "Their hearts are corrupt and determined to do evil; they create controversies all the time."

Our true identity is ultimately based on what God has done for each of us. In God, we are loved, chosen, forgiven, redeemed, and adopted.

The last stanza of the poem by Deborah Ann Belka, "Who Am I in Christ," is a fitting closing for today's devotion.

> I am sealed for the day of redemption
> I am called to eternal glory
> I am the aroma of Christ to God
> I am crucified with Christ
> I am not ashamed
> I am a sinner
> I am forgiven
> I am born again
> and I am going to heaven!
> *Who are you without Christ?*

Promises

Balancing Priorities

Squirrels can be such comical creatures. I have seen them running around the big pine trees, chasing one another. Other times I have caught them hanging on one of my bird feeders, robbing it of as much birdseed as they could. The squirrel of today's lesson however was simply sitting atop a post, a balancing act certainly.

I know about balancing acts; I perform one every day as I am sure you do too. We have many things to juggle in life: work, family, church—oftentimes in that very order. What does God's word have to say about balancing our priorities? Take a look at Matthew 6:33, where we find "But seek ye first the kingdom of God, and His righteousness; and all these things shall be added unto you." Does this mean that we will get everything we could possibly desire? No, but we will have what we need and God's blessing on our lives.

Deuteronomy 6:5 says, "And thou shalt love the Lord thy God with all thine heart, and with all thy soul, and with all thy might." If we put all this effort into loving God, it has to be our first priority. Moses goes on in the following verses to tell the children of Israel how they should teach their children the Scriptures and bind them upon their bodies so as to have access to the law of God constantly. Without studying God's word as we should, we will not love Him with all our heart, soul, and might.

What are some promises of putting God first? Philippians 4:19 tells us, "But my God shall supply all your needs according to His riches in glory by Christ Jesus." And in 2 Peter 1:4, it says, "Whereby are given unto us exceeding great and precious promises: that by these ye might be partakers of the divine nature, having escaped the corruption that is in the world through lust." And from Psalm 84:11, it states, "For the Lord God is a sun and a shield: the Lord will give grace and glory: no good thing will he withhold from them that walk uprightly."

Let's look at these three Scriptures. First, He will supply *all* our needs by His riches in glory. God's riches know no bounds. Notice, He says *all* our needs, not some of them. Secondly, we share the divine nature, which promises, at the end of our lives, we will take on immortality and live forever with the Father and Son. Lastly, He is a sun and shield; we cannot live without sun, so He is life for us. As a shield, He is our protector. The end of the verse reassures the Christian that he will hold back no good thing from them.

Mighty promises from a mighty God! Rethink your priorities, and reorder them if necessary. Don't miss out on His promises for you!

> All of God's promises have their yes in him (Christ). That is why we say Amen through him to the glory of God. (2 Corinthians 1:20)

Deeply Rooted

Recently, I was weeding the flower beds, and the Lord used the pulling of weeds to speak to me. He never ceases to amaze me in the different manners He uses to grab my attention. As I was working my way around the house, I realized that a lot of the weeds came right up with a gentle pull; others required a little more effort, while some had me pushing rocks out of the way so that I could dig my fingers into the dirt to get those stubborn ones up!

God brought the parable of the sower into my mind—you know, the seeds that fell into four different types of soil. This parable comes out of Matthew 13:3–8. Christ tells the multitude of a sower, who sowed seeds on hard, packed soil that were eaten by birds and then on a thin layer of soil over rock, and the seeds sprouted quickly, but having no root were soon scorched by the sun. Next, the seeds landed on ground infested with thorns and growth there was impossible. Finally, the seeds found good ground—they sprouted, grew, and yielded a crop. The Lord was telling me by reminding me of this scripture and giving me a tangible lesson that we, as His church, are to be like the seeds in the good ground. As I found in pulling the pesky weeds, some had taken root in good soil, and I had to really work to pull them out. We should be so rooted!

As Christians with deep roots, we hear the Word and receive it, obey, and understand, thereby manifesting Christian character and producing fruit. You may wonder about those deeply rooted weeds that did give way and come up out of the ground by my hand in comparison to being a deeply rooted true believer in Jesus Christ and possibly being plucked. Let me leave you with this thought from Romans

8:38–39: "For I am persuaded that neither death, nor life, nor angels, nor principalities, nor powers, nor things present, nor things to come, Nor height, nor depth, nor any other creature, shall be able to separate us from the love of God, which is in Christ Jesus our Lord."

If we are truly in good ground (the Word), deeply rooted by watering (Christ, the living water), and being weeded (confession and repentance), there is *nothing* that can pluck us out of His hand!

> Lord, whoever is reading this today, I pray that You help erase all doubts as it concerns this reader's faith. I believe this reader wants to draw closer to You, just like I do. As we get ready to plant our heels into the good ground, we want Your love to take root. Equip us to do the work that You called us to do and the ability to be fruit producers. Remind us daily that, as true believers, we can never be separated from Your love. In Jesus's name, amen.

Deflecting Satan's Arrows

Today, my morning devotion came from Galatians 2:15–21, and in verse 20, these words are found: "I have been crucified with Christ and I no longer live, but Christ lives in me. The life I now live in the body I live by faith in the Son of God, who loved me and gave himself for me." The writer of the devotion made a remark about how hard it is to live as Christ is in us and that it is a battle every day to do so. As I sat, pondering her remarks and this particular scripture verse, I imagined a battle in a place that I am not privy to, in a realm far beyond what I can see with human eyes—a battle between God's mighty and holy army against the enemy, the prince of this world, Satan and his demons. The angelic forces advance with shields in place; the enemy retreats while firing arrows at them, most of which are deflected into nothingness. Some, however, miss and find their targets among mankind. Those arrows may be deception, doubt, discouragement, diversion, defeat, or delay.

Especially during the Christmas season, the ending of one year and the beginning of another, I see Satan's arrows flying; however, it occurs daily. He uses this time of joy, happiness, love, and family to hit those who are bereaved, have lost jobs. Where there is sickness in the family, Satan fires his arrows, causing doubt and discouragement. He also uses the arrows of busyness to keep us from focusing on the real reason for the season—the birth of Christ, our Savior. I would encourage you to reread the story of the birth of Christ from the Gospel of Luke. Then take a look at Isaiah 9:6: "For unto us a child is born, unto us a Son is given: and the government shall be upon his shoulder; and his name shall be called Wonderful, Counsellor, The mighty God, the Everlasting Father, The Prince of Peace." Our Lord was born to die for us, to take our sins upon his shoulders, to hang upon the cross, and defeat Satan and death. He can deflect the arrows of Satan. Often it may seem impossible, but from Luke 1:37, we see this: "For with God nothing shall be impossible."

If you are experiencing any of those arrows of deception, doubt, discouragement, diversion, defeat, or delay, I pray that you will find the promise of the tiny babe born in the manger, the crucified Christ is still strong today.

Trust Him, and know the assurance of Paul as he wrote in Philippians 4:13, "I can do all things through Christ who strengtheneth me."

Jesus Christ is our only shield against Satan's arrows.

God is Always God

God is always God. This statement was used by a friend of mine in a recent sermon he preached. I scrambled for a pencil to write it down before it had a chance to slip from my mind. What a profound thought and one I don't consider often enough.

Especially in the months since the onset of COVID-19 and the subsequent shut downs, violence and various acts of hate that have been so prevalent, it is an important thing to remember. God never changes; God is always God, no matter what.

There are many mentions of the unchanging character of God in the Bible. The first reference I want to look at comes from Malachi 3:6, and it says, "I am the LORD, and I do not change; and you, children of Jacob, have not perished." Malachi was saying in this passage that Israel owes its survival entirely to the faithfulness of God. In other words, it is only His unchanging and perfect promises which have kept Israel and will keep us, as His children, as well.

Hebrews 13:8 offers this promise: "Jesus Christ is the same yesterday, today and forever." God's plan does not change. Can you imagine the extreme chaos Christians would be in if God's plan changed every time the wind changed direction? Consistency is as important for us, who are believers, as for those we will be a witness to. Chaos and confusion are of Satan; they do not come from God.

Finally, let's look at Psalm 33:11: "But the LORD's plan stands forever; what he intends to do lasts from one generation to the next." How encouraging it is to know that whatever comes in this world, (1) God is not caught unaware, and (2) His plan stands forever! The *Believer's Bible Commentary* puts it this way: "Throughout human history the ungodly have collaborated to thwart God and to ruin His people. God ultimately frustrates the cleverest plots hatched by His opponents. And nothing can hinder the accomplishment of His purposes. He will always have the last word, and whatever He plans will come to pass."

The next time something comes at you out of the blue, like gale-force winds, trying to blow you off course, remember, God is always God. There is no changing, He is immutable.

May the last stanza of M. S. Lowndes's poem, "Our God Changes Not," be both a reminder and a prayer.

> So, even though this world's unstable,
> He's still our solid rock
> And the only certainty in life,
> For our God changes not.

Guidance, Courtesy of God

Have you ever considered the direction and leading of God in your life? I will admit, all too often, I do not give it enough thought. He brought this to mind for me recently.

As I was sitting on my daughter's screened porch, enjoying a cup of coffee, one cool spring morning, I found myself watching the crows flying, breakneck speed, through the trees at the back of her yard. They were coming into the wooded area at what seemed to be top speed and not slowing down to make darts in and out of the trees. Not one of those crows hit a tree as they flew. They appeared to be guided by an unseen force.

We too are guided by an unseen force—Jesus. That is true if you are one of His children. How often do we go through life, flying as the crows at turbo speed, dodging obstacles along the way? My question now is, am I the only one to have taken my eyes off the Lord and had a collision? Can this be avoided? I would like to think that, yes, collisions with the obstacles of life can be avoided. I would like to consider that Psalm 37:23–24 gives us this truth: "The steps of a good man are ordered by the Lord: and he delighteth in his way. Though he fall, he shall not be utterly cast down: for the Lord upholdeth him with his hand." Though such a man may fall into trials and tribulations, he will never be engulfed by them, for the Lord holds him securely by His hand.

Another scriptural example that God leads us is found in Isaiah 48:17: "Thus saith the Lord, thy Redeemer, the Holy One of Israel; I am the Lord thy God which teacheth thee to profit, which leadeth thee by the way that thou shouldest go." Wow! Jehovah God, the

Creator of the earth, the sun, moon, and stars, the One by whom everything was made, loves us enough to care to teach and lead us, His children. That thought should thrill our soul!

The next time you feel that you are running or flying through life nonstop, remember that He, who holds the world in place, who sends the rain and the sun, knows exactly where you are and what obstacles you are approaching. Reconsider the words of Psalm 37, and know, without a doubt, that He is faithful to His promise, and He will hold you in His hand.

Over the Rainbow

I had planned our daughter Blair's fortieth birthday for several weeks, knowing exactly how I wanted to set up. I wanted a garden party with tables set up in front of the pond, with family eating and fellowshipping all together. The weatherman told me that Saturday was to be the best day of the weekend, and I believed him. My husband cut the grass and did the weeding around the edge of the pond. I freshened up my flowers on the patio and cleaned off the back porch in preparation for the party. Just as folks were fixing plates and heading to find their seats, the sky grew dark, and the rain began to fall…hard and fast. There went my garden party, and everyone's spirits dipped a little. We had one table we could grab fast and pull into our shop, and with other seating, everybody was able to eat inside in the dry. We were all together as I had wanted, chattering and eating, children (and dogs) were running around, playing. Okay, not too bad a party atmosphere, I decided. Then someone opened the door to see if it was still raining. Wonder of wonders, there, just over our pond, was the most glorious rainbow I'd ever seen! And the end of it was *in the pond!* Several of us ran to grab phones to capture that image permanently.

In the Scriptures, the rainbow is the sign of the promise God made to Noah after the flood, and now it was a reminder to me that God cares about even the smallest of things in our everyday lives. He knew this day was important, that this family, being together, was important. Even in my disappointment and frustration with the rain, He loved me and cared enough to show it through our rainbow.

This verse from Isaiah 54:10 comes to mind: "For the mountains shall depart and the hills be removed; but my kindness shall not depart from thee, neither shall the covenant of my peace be removed, said the Lord that hath mercy on thee." Even in the roar of chaos and upheaval, He is promising to us His kindness and mercy.

I think, usually, when we spy a rainbow, our minds go to that promise to Noah long ago, which is found in Genesis 9:15–16: "And I will remember my covenant, which is between me and you and every living creature of all flesh; and the waters shall no more become a flood to destroy all flesh. And the bow shall be in the cloud; and I will look upon it that I may remember the everlasting covenant." God is faithful to His covenant, and He is faithful in love, even in my unfaithfulness!

Perhaps you too will see an additional meaning at the next sight of a rainbow and be reminded of God's love and just how much He wants to be a part of even the little things in our lives.

The last verse of this poem by *Patricia Kubicki* sums up this devotion:

> His Rainbow of Promise is His Rainbow of love.
> Touching my heart with soft colors from above.
> A rainbow to heal me & show me "my Lord's face".
> His rainbow of love daily colors me with grace.

Protection in the Shade

A flicker of movement, a flash of color—what was it that drew my eyes to a bush at the corner of the house? I just happened by that particular window moments before on a cleaning mission, but God provided a brief interruption! In reality, I know that it wasn't happenstance that sent me in the direction of the window; God was going to give me a lesson.

This bush was full of birds! Cardinals, the bright red male and the duller-colored female, maybe a chickadee or two, and quite possibly, a few wrens made up the crowd of feathery visitors. I was surprised at the number of different birds all sharing that bush. Then as I looked further; I could see the bird feeders that hang in the Bradford pear tree were a straight shot from their vantage point in the bush. Aha, they were using my shrub as a staging area before making a fast flight to the birdseed. But why in a bush, where leaves and branches hid them from my sight so well? Protection is the answer. Camouflaged in and among the branches, they were safe from predators. This quickly brought to mind one of my favorite psalms, Psalm 91.

Psalm 91 begins like this: "Living in the Most High's shelter, camping in the Almighty's shade." Just as these birds were using my shrubbery for protection, we can do the same in our walk with God. Our heavenly Father offers us protection against our adversary, the devil. By living and walking with Christ as our Savior, we find refuge and protection under His wings (vs 4).

Did I mention how much I love this psalm? Look on to verses 14–16, and make this a personal prayer. I marked up my Bible some years back, and I write here as I read it each and every time.

> Because Lucy hath set her love upon me, therefore will I deliver her; I will set her on high, because she hath known my name. She shall call upon me, and I will answer her: I will be with her in trouble; I will deliver her and honour her. With long life will I satisfy her and shew her my salvation."

Is this not a beautiful promise? Make it your own, and pray it back to God when you have your devotional time.

Remember the scene of the birds in the bush? Our Creator provided that shelter for our feathered friends, but He so much more desires to care for you. We are taught this in Matthew 10:29–31, and as you read that passage, let the last line really sink in: "You are worth more than many sparrows."

Taste and See

This morning, my grandson and I took a little walk before the day grew too hot. We wandered by the tractor shed and up past the grapevine to a place where I had spotted a bit of honeysuckle a few days earlier. Nothing says summer to me like the scent of honeysuckle! Then there is that little dollop of sweetness, just waiting inside the bloom! I pulled a few blooms from the stem and let Bryson get a taste of that goodness. He was a little unsure until that first drop hit his tongue, and then he wanted more and more. In a matter of a minute or so, we had "eaten" six or eight of them, and still he asked for more. That is how life lived walking with Jesus should be; we should want more day by day.

"Taste and see how good the Lord is! The one who takes refuge in him is truly happy!" This comes from Psalm 34:8. A good explanation of the verse is found on *gotquestions.org* and is "to taste involves testing or sampling; to see involves understanding or perceiving." The phrase "taste and see" then means "try and experience." David urges God's people to discover the goodness of the Lord by personal trial and experience it for themselves. He doesn't want readers to merely take his word for it that the Lord is good; he wants them to actively experience and know for themselves the fact that God is good.

Further into this same passage, we see that those who trust and take refuge in Him have every need met (vs 9–10). In verses 11–15, we find that He provides a long and good life and delivers us from troubles and enemies in the final verses (17–22). What has He not covered? If we place our trust and hope in the Lord, then He will supply *all* of our needs. Philippians 4:19 verifies this truth: "My God will meet your every need out of his riches in the glory that is found in Christ Jesus."

Hebrews 6:4–5 attests to the "wanting more" after that first taste, "because it's impossible to restore people to changed hearts and lives who turn away once they have seen the light, tasted the heavenly gift, become partners with the Holy Spirit, and tasted God's good word (and the powers of the coming age)."

Yes, the honeysuckle is sweet, but nothing can compare to the sweetness of having Jesus as your Savior! Taste and test, see and understand, and experience God's goodness for yourself!

Taste and see…
And but believe that
He holds riches in glory for you and me.

Taste and see…
He will meet every need
For those who will plead
To step into the Light
Out of darkness and restored of sight.
Taste and see…
How good is He
Who is our refuge and our might!

Truly Committed

Like most grandmothers, I sing to my grandbabies when I rock them. I'm certain that a variety of songs are sung by parents and grandparents alike. I generally sing hymns. I don't have the voice to sing in the choir, so I sing to the children who aren't yet old enough to wrinkle a nose or grimace at my "make a joyful noise" attempts. Today, a chorus kept running around in my head, although I couldn't identify it immediately, it's message hit home.

Do you recognize this chorus? "But I know Whom I have believed, and am persuaded that He is able to keep that which I've committed unto Him against that day." What? Committed? I am to have committed something to Christ, but have I? I committed my life at thirteen years of age, but boy oh boy, did I have a lot to learn about commitment!

God wants us to commit *all* to him. Along with our heart, He expects His children to commit their finances, family, and work to Him. I must confess that I have not done a great job at this thing called commitment to Christ. Oftentimes, I try to fix the situation myself. Oh, I may whisper a "please, Lord, help me with this" type of prayer, but Jesus wants us to be more hands off than hands on!

With all this thought of commitment, exactly what does the word mean? *Webster* describes it as (1) a promise to do or give something, (2) a promise to be loyal to someone or something, and (3) the attitude of someone who works very hard to do or support something. Wow, each definition here could apply to spiritual commitment. Initially, as a new Christian, we make the promise to give something (our hearts and lives) and to be loyal to our commitment to Christ. Finally, we work hard in our new life and show the world where we stand in faith (support).

This commitment is biblical as we find in 1 Kings 8:61, "Now may you be committed to the Lord our God with all your heart by following his laws and observing his commands." When we commit our lives to the Lord, He will bless our efforts according to His perfect will in ways beyond our understanding. We should serve the Lord faithfully and then leave the results to Him. Though we will still face times of difficulty, we can trust that God is working for His ultimate good—and ours—through our efforts to please Him in our daily vocation.

Psalm 37:5–6 says, "Commit your way to the Lord! Trust Him! He will act and will make your righteousness shine like the dawn." What a promise! It is our job to trust Him, and He will uphold His commitment to His children.

Will you pray with me today?

> Father God, help me to make that commitment
> today that You so desire from me. Give me
> grace to maintain my commitment and faith
> to know You will keep it until that day.

Oh, and for those who may still be wondering the name of the hymn I couldn't pin down...it is "I Know Whom I Have Believed" by Marshall Hall.

Salvation

Enter the Narrow Gate

Just when I thought the pollen season was over, there it was again! Not as thick and yellow as earlier in the spring, however there was a light dusting of it on the pond. The pattern it created reminded me of one of those simple circular mazes that you might see in the newspaper or a children's magazine, the object being to find the way out in one continuous path. The image didn't last long. Once the wind blew across the pond's surface, the movement of the water created a different pattern. That was all right; God had already planted a thought in my brain.

Life is a maze rarely, if ever, completed in a continuous forward movement. More often than not, there are wrong turns, reverse moves, and U-turns. This applies to our spiritual life as well. We know from the Scriptures that the right path is narrow, and few find it. "Go in through the narrow gate. The gate that leads to destruction is broad and the road wide, so many people enter through it. But the gate that leads to life is narrow and the road difficult, so few people find it" (Matthew 7:13–14).

We have a choice to make in life, one that will lead to destruction or eternal life with our Creator. God's goodness and mercy are what lead one through that narrow gate. What happens once inside the gate on the difficult road? It is not a cakewalk, and although we make the choice to walk through the narrow gate, we take each subsequent step in faith. Only because Jesus died on the cross for all sinners are we able to walk it daily in faith.

What if, like a maze on paper, we choose a dead end or a path that leads us back to the beginning? What if we take a misstep on the road, get sidetracked? We need only to ask forgiveness for making the wrong choice or bad decision. God's Word tells us that He will forgive confessed sin. First John 1:9 says this: "But if we confess our sins, He is faithful and just to forgive us our sins and cleanse us from everything we've done wrong."

Go ahead, step through the narrow gate, daily do your best to not have to make a U-turn, but know and believe that if you do, Jesus pleads our case if we will only confess it and repent.

Life can be a maze, but we have a shepherd to lead us down the pathway.

Granddaddy's Jesus

This past Memorial Day found Brooks and me in the cooler temperatures of the North Carolina mountains and the home of our son, daughter-in-love, and precious granddaughter, Amelia. On our last afternoon there, we went to the local park, which just happens to border the river. Naturally, Brooks and Gregory took fishing rods and related paraphernalia for trout fishing, while Amelia bounced from swing to slide and back again. Nicole and I also bounced from swing to slide and back again, just trying to keep up with her boundless energy!

Amelia is two, so she has that pure innocence and unquestioning trust that Jesus declares we must have in order to come into His kingdom. And calling to him a child, he put him in the midst of them and said, "Truly, I say to you, unless you turn and become like children, you will never enter the kingdom of heaven" (Matthew 18:2–3 ESV).

After our park adventure, we decided to grab a bite to eat before heading back to the house. Once we were seated in the restaurant, Amelia wanted to sit between Grandma and Granddaddy, and again her ability to bounce was confirmed as she moved from me to Brooks and back again! As she was sitting with Brooks, she spied his cross necklace, which had worked its way above the neckline of his shirt. She proceeded to pull it out completely to discover Jesus on the cross. When asked who it was on the cross, she answered, "Granddaddy's Jesus." I thought immediately, there's my next devotion!

The gospel message is so simple that children can understand it—believe and be saved. It's we adults that want to make it hard to understand, how can we be loved and desired by God? Oftentimes, we think we have to fix ourselves, correct whatever is wrong with us, in order for us to be accepted by the Lord. It is a gift, and all we need to do is accept it. Ephesians 2:8–9 says, "For by grace you have been saved through faith. And this is not your own doing; it is the gift of God, not a result of works, so that no one may boast" (ESV).

So going back to the main theme here of Granddaddy's Jesus may bring the question of how to have a personal relationship with Jesus. The Scriptures tell us to receive (accept) and believe. We find this truth in John 1:12: "But to all who did receive him, who believed in his name, he gave the right to become children of God" (ESV). The next steps are studying His Word and praying.

Today, you too can know Amelia's Granddaddy's Jesus, "for God so loved the world that He gave His only begotten Son that whosoever believeth on Him should not perish but have everlasting life" (John 3:16).

Ask Jesus into your heart, and begin or refresh your relationship with Him.

Heaven or Hell?

With the onset of warmer weather recently, my husband has been able to do what he has hoped to do for a long time—fish with the grandchildren. He has talked about how much he wanted to teach them to fish since, well since they were too little to even hold a rod. As with any fisherman, you keep some, and you toss some back. The fish good enough for eating are kept, and those that are either too small or just not good meat to eat are thrown back. Any way this is done, it separates the good fish from the bad.

Jesus even used fishing to teach His followers in the Parable of the Net. In Matthew 13:47–50, He speaks about the kingdom of heaven in comparison to the fisherman pulling in a net full of a variety of fish. The good ones were put aside for later use, while the bad ones were thrown away. Where I want to focus with this devotion is the last portion of the passage, verses 49–50: "That's the way it will be at the end of the present age. The angels will go out and separate the evil people from the righteous people, and will throw the evil ones into a burning furnace. People there will be weeping and grinding their teeth."

There are many in today's world that do not believe in a literal place of torment, eternal separation from God that we know of as hell. If you believe the Bible is the inspired and inerrant word of God, if you believe that it is His truth, then you must believe in hell. This is not a place anyone should want to spend eternity.

I can't even put into words how awful I imagine the eternal sound of one's own weeping and gnashing of teeth would be. Let's look at the definitions for these words from *Webster's Dictionary*. *Weeping* means tearful; plain and simple tears into infinity. A synonym I noticed was bowed as a weeping willow tree branch, so my mind's eye pictured someone bent and crying nonstop. Most crying also comes with moans and wails, so add that to the image. *Webster* defines grinding as it relates to teeth as pressing together with a rotating motion. Again, a motion that is set to never end.

If you are reading this and are not saved by grace through faith in Jesus Christ, I present you with Romans 10:9–10, 13: "If you confess with your mouth Jesus is Lord and in your heart you have faith that God raised him from the dead, you will be saved. Trusting with the heart leads to righteousness, and confessing with the mouth leads to salvation. All who call on the Lord's name will be saved."

What do you have to lose? Eternity is forever, and we will spend it in a glorious place with God and His Son, Jesus, or in this terrible place of eternal torment. The decision is yours. Which place will you choose?

> We are all destined for one place or the other
> There is no place in-between to run for cover
> We must decide now where we intend to stay
> We cannot be fence-sitters come judgment day.
> (Ellen Bailey)

Your Name, Not a Blank

Blank, empty space, and void of your name—is this what anyone really wants to see, looking into the Book of Life? As my husband and I were discussing some points from Revelation recently, he read this statement to me from his Bible in a footnote by Reverend C. I. Scofield: "The book of life is there to answer such as plead their works for justification—an awful blank where the name might have been." Boy, does that get your attention!

In Matthew 7:22–23, we find the following: "On the Judgment Day, many people will say to me "Lord, Lord, didn't we prophesy in your name and expel demons in your name and do lots of miracles in your name? Then I will tell them, I've never known you. Get away from me, you people who do wrong." I cannot imagine hearing those words. However, this passage does make one think about knowing for sure if your name is written in the Book of Life.

In my study for this devotion, I found five characteristics that are found in the believer. I have titled them the five Cs of a Christian. The first C is *confession*. First John 5:1 says, "Everyone who believes that Jesus is the Christ has been born from God." You must first believe, and you have to confess Jesus as Lord.

Change is the second C. From 1 John 2:29, we read, "If you know that he is righteous, you also know that every person who practices righteousness is born from him." When we are saved by Jesus, it changes how we act, speak, and think.

For the third C, we have *compassion*. Love is an often-repeated theme in 1 John; therefore, we look to 1 John 4:7 for this reference:

"Dear friends, let's love each other, because love is from God, and everyone who loves is born from God, and knows God."

The fourth C is *conflict*. We face plenty of conflict in the world. We have an adversary that we must struggle to overcome, but we also have a promise that we will achieve the victory. Look at 1 John 5:4: "Because everyone who is born from God defeats the world. And this is the victory that has defeated the world: our faith."

The fifth and final C is *conduct*. "Those born from God don't practice sin because God's DNA remains in them. They can't sin because they are born from God" (1 John 3:9). I would like to clarify this using the explanation I read by Dr. David Jeremiah. He states, "John is not saying that whoever sins once is not born of God. That would disqualify all of us. It would certainly disqualify me. But John is saying, in effect, 'Whoever keeps on willfully sinning, violating God's law with stubborn disregard and ongoing wickedness, cannot have assurance of salvation.'"

As I said above, I can't imagine looking into that great book and seeing a huge blank space where my name could have been. If you are reading this today and are not saved, take steps to ensure you do find your name in the Book of Life before it is too late.

> That day we stand before *Him*
> They will call out each name shown.
> If your name isn't listed…
> Your opportunity has flown.
>
> To be included in this book,
> Should be your chief desire.
> If your name is not recorded…
> You'll be cast into the fire.
> C. C.

About the Author

Lucy Allen is the author of *The Pond*, a devotional book, published in 2016 by CFP and is a resident of NC. Lucy is married to her high school sweetheart, and they have just celebrated forty-six years of marriage. She and her husband, Brooks, have two children and two grandchildren. Lucy is a member of Crestview Baptist Church, where she has served in a number of capacities over the years.

At the onset of the COVID-19 pandemic in 2020, Lucy's church started a website to unite the congregation during the months that they could not meet and worship in person. Since 2020, Lucy has been one of three contributing authors providing daily devotions.

Lucy has also had works published in online publications ChristianDevotions.us and AwakeOurHearts.com.

Printed in the USA
CPSIA information can be obtained
at www.ICGtesting.com
JSHW020713111023
49721JS00002B/11